GHOST STORIES

STORIES

of

AMERICA

Dan Asfar & Edrick Thay

GHOST HOUSE

Ghost House Boo

The Publisher: Ghost House Books
Distributed by Lone Pine Publishing
10145 – 81 Avenue
Edmonton, AB T6E 1W9
Canada
Website: http://www.ghostbooks.net

National Library of Canada Cataloguing in Publication Data
Asfar, Dan, 1973–
    Ghost stories of America
    ISBN 1-894877-11-X

    1. Ghosts—United States. 2. Legends—United States. I. Thay,
Edrick, 1977– II. Title.
GR105.5.A83 2002   398.2'0973'05   C2002-910730-X

Editorial Director: Nancy Foulds
Project Editors: Shelagh Kubish, Chris Wangler
Researcher: Alana Bevans
Illustrations Coordinator: Carol Woo
Production Coordinator: Jennifer Fafard
Book Design, Layout & Production: Elliot Engley
Cover Design: Gerry Dotto

Photo Credits: Every effort has been made to accurately credit photographers. Any errors or omissions should be directed to the publisher for changes in future editions. The photographs in this book are reproduced with the kind permission of the following sources:
    Library of Congress HABS, ALA, 46–DEMO, 1–5 (p.15), HABS, ALA, 46–DEMO, 1–26 (p.17), HABS, DEL, 1–DOV, 6–1 (p.20), HABS, DEL, 1–DOV, 6–5 (p.23), USZ62–28258 (p.26), HABS, KY, 76–WHAL, 1–3 (p.29), HABS, MASS, 5–SAL, 19–1 (p.37), HABS, MASS, 5–SAL, 19–8 (p.42), HABS, DC, WASH, 8–20 (p.48), HABS, DC, WASH, 8–29 (p.51), HABS, NY, 31–NEYO, 3–1 (p.63), HABS, WYO, 8–FOLA, 3E–1 (p.95), USZ62–100354 (p.96), HABS, WYO, 8–FOLA,3E–4 (p.98), USZ62–128414 (p.114–15), HABS, OHIO, 31–CINT, 5–6 (p.163), HABS, OHIO, 31–CINT, 5–1 (p.166), USZ62–104482 (p.176), USZ62–108225 (p.179), D4–22686 (p.188b), USZ62–116074 (p.193), USZ62–91077 (p.239); Local History Department, Grand Rapids Local Library (p.73), New Orleans Public Library, Louisiana Division, recent 662 (p.77), Richard Federici (p.85), from *The American West in the Nineteenth Century,* 1992, Dover Publications, (p.104), National Archives of Canada C–28599 (p.121), C–1843 (p.188a); La Posada de Sante Fe (p.128), Museum of New Mexico, negative #11040 (p.131), Forepaugh's Restaurant, St. Paul (p.133), Biltmore Hotel (p.146, p.149), Glenbow Archives Calgary, Canada, NA–1700–10 (p.172), Daniel Ter-Nedden/Ghosttowngallery.com (p.206), University of Notre Dame Archives GNEG12B/43 (p.218).

The stories, folklore and legends in this book are based on the authors' research of sources including individuals whose experiences have led them to believe they have encountered phenomena of some kind or another. They are meant to entertain, and neither the publisher nor the authors claim these stories represent fact.

We acknowledge the financial support of the Government of Canada through the Book Publishing Industry Development Program (BPIDP) for our publishing activities.

PC: P5

Dedication

To all the storytellers

Contents

Chapter 4: Spirits on the Menu

Chapter 5: Haunted by History

Chapter 6: Cemeteries

Chapter 7: Haunted Universities

Chapter 8: Frightening Folklore

Acknowledgments

Many thanks go to those who stoke and feed the ghost story tradition, those who have sought out the unexplained and the unusual and who have worked to illuminate the world of shadows. Thank you to Charles Adams III, Dennis William Hauck, Earl Murray, Michael Norman, Janice Oberding, Jack Powell, Nancy Roberts, Bill Samuels, Beth Scott and L.B. Taylor, Jr. Without their curiosities, this book would have suffered.

The in-house staff at Ghost House Books provided constant support and invaluable advice throughout the writing of this book, but the writing is but one step in the creation of a book. For her patience in and dedication to making our jobs easier, we owe a debt of thanks to researcher Alana Bevan. For their sure-handed and insightful editing, Chris Wangler and Shelagh Kubish have our gratitude. Without you, *Ghost Stories of America* would be a lesser book. For her skill in obtaining the images that breathe life into our text, Carol Woo has our deepest appreciation. For their work in creating and crafting a presentation at once familiar and unique for the book, Elliot Engley and Gerry Dotto have our thanks.

And finally, a special thank you to Nancy Foulds and Shane Kennedy, whose faith and support throughout this project have been unwavering and invaluable.

Introduction

Ghost, phantom, apparition, specter, revenant, shade, wraith—many words in the English language describe entities that exist outside the sensory pale. And for those who are inclined to dwell on the subject, there are many theories regarding what these entities are. For as long as humans have been able to communicate their thoughts, the inexplicable shapes dwelling at the edge of darkness have been recurring themes in literature and folklore. Strange sounds in the night, cold hands grasping at warm throats and forces beyond human control or understanding—since time immemorial, these encounters with the unknown have been part of the human experience.

Yet while supernatural occurrences continue to affect countless people in society today, the subject of ghosts is largely rebuffed by the predominant rationalism of our age. Supernatural phenomena, taken seriously only by a small number of legitimate researchers, largely serve as entertainment in the social media, as moviegoers and book readers alike look for that peculiar kind of joy that comes with the fearful thrill of a good ghost story.

We shouldn't lose sight of the fact, however, that paranormal occurrences are a very real part of many Americans' lives. Every day, people across the country cope with bizarre incidents that contradict the laws of nature. Transparent apparitions, sentient mists, disembodied voices, invisible physical forces—these are just a few of the supernatural occurrences that are reported from the rocky promontories of Maine to the sandy beaches of California.

There is no shortage of supernatural accounts in the United States. While we, the authors, were limited to one story per state in the following volume, our researcher, Alana Bevan, quickly realized that there is an almost limitless number of tales to pick from for every state. Hauntings are not limited to houses and cemeteries; indeed, there are so many supernatural tales to be told in the States that one might conclude the whole nation is haunted to one degree or another.

Such a broad and dramatic statement might elicit strong responses. Disregard, for a moment, the natural skepticism that usually accompanies any affirmation of the paranormal. The idea that we are living in a world populated by the unseen dead, that we are conducting our daily business alongside phantom citizens from a long-forgotten past, must call into question the way we perceive our own realities.

For instance, the conventional wisdom that the world today can be better understood through the lens of its history does not make room for the idea that long-deceased historical personalities are observing *us* through this same lens. While all of us are familiar with the idea of the everlasting soul and the religious concept of life after death, those of us who believe in such things tend to separate the essences of the living from the dead: we are *here*, they are *there*. But there are many among us who are inclined to believe otherwise.

Millions of people throughout the United States have had experiences that suggest the dead haven't made it too far from the places they knew while they were alive. Apparitions, disembodied sounds, moving objects—there is almost always a story associated with these phenomena, tragic, morbid or memorable pasts that account for the bizarre sights and sounds afflicting haunted areas today.

What follows is an exposition of some of the more famous supernatural tales that have emerged from the United States. Included are local legends that are well known to paranormal enthusiasts of the respective states, hauntings that are a result of horrible tragedies still unforgotten and supernatural stories connected to prominent citizens who made significant contributions to their world when they were living.

So sit back, turn the lights down low and prepare to delve into the dark parallel history of the United States. Where long-dead leading citizens continue to roam their halls of power, past tragedies continue to play themselves out in the bumps and shadows of the night and mortal obsessions find channel in the spirits of those unfortunate Americans who were possessed by them while they lived. These are the ghost stories of America, the celebrations and lamentations of our past, told through the spirits that continue to haunt us today.

1
Historic
Homes

KANSAS
Atchison's Haunted House

Around Atchison, she is called Sallie the Man-Hater. A vicious specter that haunts a stately centennial home on the west bank of the Missouri River, Sallie has become a supernatural celebrity in Kansas in recent years. She has appeared on a number of local television programs, makes headlines in the newspaper every Halloween and is the focus of many of the state's paranormal enthusiasts. But for those few who have actually had the misfortune of living with Sallie, the malevolent spirit is neither an interesting conversation piece nor a subject for study, but a bad memory that should be forgotten as soon as possible.

Many have been misled by Sallie's moniker. A man-hater she may be, yet Sallie is not the spirit of a jilted lover, embittered wife or vengeful matriarch. In fact, Sallie is only a child—probably a frightened, angry one who still cannot understand why she never made it past her seventh birthday. She has been known to take out all her fear, anger and uncertainty on certain men who dare set foot in the house in which she died.

Sallie's story reaches back to the early 1900s. It was early one spring morning, and Atchison's premier physician was enjoying breakfast in his home as he looked out on the waters of the Missouri. Whatever thoughts he was immersed in were interrupted by a panicked knocking at his door. Getting up to see who it was, he instantly snapped into his medical mindframe when his eyes fell on the two humble forms at his front door. A tear-faced mother, sobbing in frantic concern, stood there with her young daughter in her arms. The girl was obviously in extreme pain, clutching her abdomen and letting out long, agonized wails as she twitched convulsively. Her name was Sallie.

Without missing a beat, the doctor picked the young girl up, took her to his office and laid her down on his examination table. He arrived at his diagnosis in minutes: the girl had appendicitis, and her appendix was about to rupture. Quickly anesthetizing her with a facemask soaked in ether, he brought out his surgical tools for an emergency operation. He already had his scalpel in hand and was beginning to cut when he heard the girl emit a weak scream. Looking up, he saw that she was staring down at him as he cut; she was obviously horrified and was trying hard to get up, but between the drugs and the pain was unable. Since the doctor deemed her condition too grave to delay treatment, he proceeded with the surgery, though his patient lay watching in bewildered terror. Alas, the doctor's urgency was well founded, and the girl's appendix ruptured before he was able to remove it. She was dead before the day was up.

For reasons unknown, the doctor moved out of his home soon after Sallie was buried, and for a long time after that, little was said of the incident or of the house that it occurred in. The tragedy of young Sallie receded into local history, and it wasn't until the early 1990s that Sallie's story returned to Atchison with a bloody vengeance.

A family that had just moved into the house began having disturbing experiences. Or rather, the man in the small family began having disturbing experiences. Neither mother nor daughter was ever touched; at no time did the females of the house feel in danger or even slightly out of place, though the strange events that occurred early on in the haunting were unsettling to all.

The television would turn on in the middle of the night. When the husband and wife would get up, they would find only the family dog in the room, its hackles up, growling at the wall as if preparing to attack somebody neither of them could see. While they succeeded for a while at blaming the trouble with the television on the dog, they had no way of explaining the family portraits, which were continually flipped around so they hung upside down on the walls. This would usually happen some time in the middle of the day when nobody was home. And then there were their daughter's toys. Whenever they were strewn about, they were always found shortly after, arranged into a perfect circle on the floor.

But these could all qualify as supernatural pranks; it wasn't until the attacks began that things got really out of hand. The man of the house could feel the change in his bones. One day, the house just got cold and it never got warmer. Though his wife and daughter didn't complain, the husband could never get comfortable. When he wasn't struggling with the constant temperature drop, he was fighting off the butterflies in his stomach, feeling as if someone was going to hit him at any time. Sure enough, the attacks began shortly thereafter.

He was in a first-floor room the first time it happened. His stomach had just started its familiar adrenaline-fueled churning when he felt a painful rake across his forearm. The man looked down to see three long gashes running down his arm. Over the next few months, the attacks continued. Sometimes he would feel the slashing across the back; on other occasions, he would double over as three cuts made their way across his stomach. Rest grew increasingly difficult. Strange dreams would often interrupt feverish sleep, and more than once he would wake to see a glowering young girl standing at the foot of his bed, staring at him silently.

That was when the family decided to move. The popular belief is that the girl was Sallie, who was also responsible for the attacks on the father. If this is true, Sallie is a lonely spirit, unable to understand why she had to die and why she was subjected to so much pain before she passed away. It's possible that her experience on the operating table has caused her to take her anger out on *all* men. The only problem with this explanation is that no stories have emerged from the house since the family moved away. Though other families have moved in since—some including men—no bizarre events or malicious attacks have been reported. Maybe the man who was attacked bore a striking resemblance to the doctor in question. It could also be that Sallie was waiting for the 90-year anniversary of her death to arrive, and is quiet once again. Who knows? All that is certain is that the house in Atchison became famous in the early 1990s, and there are many supernatural buffs who are waiting for young Sallie to strike again.

ALABAMA
Gaineswood

One of the finest examples of antebellum Southern architecture can be found in Demopolis. Gaineswood is a beautiful Greek Revival mansion that has been carefully preserved by the Alabama Historic Commission. The past has been faithfully recreated in Gaineswood, right down to the presence of a woman who died in the home many, many years ago.

Visitors will find the home still decorated with its original furnishings, and should they linger before the grand rosewood piano donated in 1976, they might be treated to a concert of sorts, a concert the likes of which most have never seen, for there is no performer—at least not one visible.

Demopolis was founded in 1817 by a group of political exiles from France, who had fled the country when Napoleon

Gaineswood: a hauntingly beautiful Alabama mansion

abdicated in 1814. The settlers were helped in its initial development by General George Strother Gaines, a Choctaw Indian agent. Gaines became Demopolis' first documented property owner. On his 480 acres Gaines built a cabin, but by 1831, Gaines felt that a change was needed and he moved to Mobile.

For 12 years, Gaines held onto his property. In 1843, General Nathan Bryan Whitfield, a grower of king cotton in North Carolina, purchased the land. Over the next 18 years, in what can only be described as a labor of love, Gaines' once-humble cabin was expanded. Working from his own designs, Whitfield assembled a small army of laborers, artisans, skilled slaves and craftsmen to create a mansion complete with a grand Corinthian ballroom and an Ionic parlor. When everything was completed in 1861, Whitfield took pride in his achievement.

Its construction was not free of disappointment, however. In 1846, Whitfield's wife, Betsy, the mother of his 12 children, fell ill and passed away. Charged with the care of his burgeoning brood, Whitfield set about finding a governess for his children. Of all the applicants who presented themselves to Whitfield, Evelyn Carter was the most impressive. She was hired and while she could not be expected to fully replace Betsy, the children took to Carter. Like an antebellum Mary Poppins, Carter brought a semblance of joy back into the Whitfield home, entertaining the family nightly with recitals in the home. Some nights, she played the piano. On others, it was the flute or the violin. But the most magical nights were when Carter sang and the home was filled with the soaring melodies of her beautiful voice. These were happy times in Gaineswood, but they would come to a quick and unexpected end.

Carter fell ill and with her dying breaths, she begged Whitfield to take her body back to her home in Virginia, to

A ghostly governess returned to play the piano at Gaineswood, bringing music and joy back to the house.

be buried alongside her family. Whitfield promised to fulfill this task to the best of his abilities, but he could not keep his promise. Winter had already fallen and had rendered the dirt roads muddy and impossible to travel. The railroad didn't reach Demopolis for at least another year, in 1862. Travel on the rivers was treacherous. Whitfield had no choice but to seal his former governess' body in a pine casket and store it underneath the cellar steps until the spring.

Carter was missed. The house sat silent as a gloom settled over the rooms like a blanket of dust. So, one can imagine the Whitfields' surprise when, one night, Carter sang again. From beneath the cellar steps came Carter's unmistakably beautiful voice, singing the songs that had served so recently to brighten the heart and fortify the spirit. Unable to return home, Carter had chosen to do what she could do for the family from beyond the grave. Her footsteps could be heard padding around the piano, at which point the piano would play by itself. Carter may have been dead in body, but her spirit was quite determinedly alive.

With spring's arrival, Carter's body was moved to her family's burial ground in Virginia. But the paranormal events continued to occur. Even though she lay in rest in the east, Carter's ghost remained active in Gaineswood, moving about the home as if death had never come. She continued to serenade the family, and the children could hear the sounds of her silk skirts brushing against the walls and her soft footsteps.

Even after the Whitfields came and went, the home continued to be the site of eerie recitals. In the 1970s, restoration workers were working late into the evening when they heard the piano playing. When they went to check on the instrument, they found nobody sitting at its keys. And on those quiet nights when the wind is still, the moon is full and the smell of absolute calm is in the air, people still claim they can hear Evelyn Carter's voice rising from beneath Gaineswood's cellar steps.

DELAWARE
Woodburn

Delaware Governor Charles Terry was sitting at the dining room table alone, looking over policy documents. It was late in the evening, and the governor was winding down, sipping a glass of Bordeaux as he read. It was past midnight when his eyes began to grow heavy. Calling it a night, he emptied his glass, gathered up his papers and pushed himself to his feet, starting for the luxurious bedroom of the 18th-century Woodburn house. Governor Terry was almost out of the opulent dining room when he suddenly remembered that he had forgotten to do something. Turning around and walking back to the table, the governor grabbed a clean wine glass, uncorked the bottle of Bordeaux and poured another glass of the rich red wine. That done, he walked out of the dining room, up the stairs and crawled into bed, leaving behind the two wine glasses, one empty, one full.

The first rays of sunlight spilling through the mansion's enormous windows the next morning illuminated both glasses, exactly where the governor had placed them; the only difference was that both glasses were empty.

The year was 1966, and Charles Terry was the first Delaware governor to reside in the Woodburn house after it had been purchased by the state in 1965. The ghost haunting the magnificent Georgian mansion had been a staple in Delaware's folklore for over a century, but it wasn't until the house was declared the official governor's residence that new life was breathed into the old legend of the ghost of Woodburn.

The legend began in 1790, when Charles Hillyard, a cantankerous patriarch who ruled his family of 10 children like a

Woodburn, now the state governor's residence, is the site of many strange and ghostly events.

despot, financed the construction of the Woodburn mansion in Dover, Delaware. Very little flattering information has survived about Hillyard's character. Folklore has painted him as an eccentric tyrant who drank too much, delighted in the suffering of others and demanded complete control over his children's lives. One account has him lounging in the Woodburn great hall with a bottle of fine wine, watching his 10 offspring closely as they stood barefoot on their tiptoes in front of him. He forced them to stand there for hours and whipped their feet with a riding crop when their toes finally lost strength and they fell back on their feet.

Another story has Hillyard chasing one of his sons, Charles Jr., through the grounds with a loaded pistol when the young man told him that he intended to move to New

York and become a writer. Legend has it that in the chase around the gardens, Hillyard fired at his son several times, almost killing him on the front porch of the mansion. It is said that the young man would've certainly gotten a bullet in the head if he hadn't slammed the door behind him as he ran inside; he owed his life to the thick wooden door that stopped the well-aimed bullet from finding its mark. Workers renovating Woodburn in 1998 were stripping paint off the northern porch door when they discovered a small hole under the layers of paint that had accumulated over the years. Located over five feet from the ground and reaching about halfway through the door, the single perforation could have easily been a bullet hole, fired by an enraged father at his fleeing son.

The bizarre occurrences that have long been reported in the mansion are definitely worthy of such a demented founder. Charles Hillyard made his first postmortem appearance in Woodburn in 1815, one year after he had passed away. His daughter Mary purchased the house with her husband, Dr. Martin Bates, after Mr. Hillyard passed on. From the very day they moved in, Mary struggled with a feeling that she was living under the disapproving eye of her father. It did not help that she often spied a figure moving in the periphery of her vision—a man in colonial dress wearing a powdered wig, knee high britches and hose. Whenever she turned to look directly at the man hovering at the edge of her vision, he would vanish into thin air. He never remained long enough for her to get a good look, but the cold feeling in the pit of her stomach suggested that the presence was none other than the spirit of her father.

Her fears were confirmed one dark fall morning when the Bates family was entertaining an itinerant clergyman named Lorenzo Dow. Martin Bates, Mary and Reverend Dow were in the dining room about to begin breakfast when Reverend Dow interrupted, asking if they weren't going to wait for the other guest. Mrs. Bates' stomach jumped into her throat. "What other guest?"

Reverend Dow told her of the elderly man he had passed when he was coming downstairs for dinner. Mary was frantic. "What did he look like?" she asked. The description Reverend Dow gave matched her father identically.

Years passed, and little was recorded about the elderly man who refused to leave Woodburn. Judge George Fisher was the owner of Woodburn over half a century later, in 1870, when the next bizarre occurrence was recorded in the folklore of the house. Judge Fisher's son, George Jr., who was home from college for Christmas break, had brought a friend home to stay for the holidays.

It happened on the first night the two students were in Woodburn. Fisher's young friend was given the guest room, which had been Charles Hillyard's room years before. When the student walked into his room, he found the fireplace in full blaze. He was surprised because it was late and all the servants had retired some time before. But when his eyes caught the figure of a man reclining in the chair facing the fire, his heart jumped. The chair's back was facing him, so he couldn't be sure who was sitting in it, but the sudden wave of irrational fear that washed over the young man warned him that he was looking on something that wasn't of this world.

His worst fears were realized when the figure suddenly leaned over the armrest and stared straight at him. It was an old man dressed in 18th-century attire, with a deeply wrinkled face the color of worn paper. The two stared at each other for seconds before the man's deathly pale face broke into a hideous grin; that was when the young guest screamed and fainted in fear. The room was completely dark when

It appears that the demanding Charles Hillyard continues to visit the mansion he had built.

George Jr. rushed in after he heard his friend fall. He was puzzled by the story his friend told after he was revived, for there was no fire burning in the room, and nobody was sitting in the plush armchair before the fireplace.

Strange happenings continued in the Woodburn house. Dr. Frank Hall, who lived in the house during much of the first half of the 20th century, was the first to notice the dead resident's appreciation for fine wine. Bottles of the house best were regularly found empty in the wine cellar, though the corks were intact and the seals unbroken.

Governor Charles Terry was the first resident to actively accommodate the spirit of Woodburn's founder. Being told of Hillyard's taste for alcohol, he made it a habit to leave a glass of his finest red on the dining room table before he went to bed. Every morning, without exception, the glass would be found emptied.

To this day, strange things continue to transpire at the Woodburn house. Workers who have been hired to do minor repairs have heard whispers coming from nowhere in the hallways. Security guards report the sound of footsteps in the front hall on the ground floor. Thorough investigations of the hall have never revealed the source of these phantom footsteps, even when they've been heard walking through the house several times in an evening. And then there are the stores of wine that continue to be emptied from Woodburn's cellar. It seems that the spirit of Hillyard has retained some memory of his terrestrial appetites long after his material form has ceased to be. Yet given the relative benevolence of his haunting, it might be said that the passage of years after his death assuaged the cruel nature he was infamous for while alive.

KENTUCKY
White Hall Mansion

His is a famous name, but this Cassius Clay was not a boxer. He was a politician, a man who fought his battles not for belts and titles, but for the hearts and minds of the people in the war to save a nation.

Cassius Marcellus Clay was born in 1810 to Revolutionary War veteran Green Clay and his wife, Sallie Clay. He was born in Clermont, the Clays' plantation home in Madison County, Kentucky. Clermont, which came to be known as White Hall, was also the site of Cassius Clay's death in 1903. He was born there, died there and some reports indicate that this important American figure haunts the place still.

When young Cassius Clay attended Yale, he quickly learned that he was quite different from other southerners there. Southerners had been attracted to the Ivy League school since southern idol John C. Calhoun had graduated from the institution in 1804. A society of southerners, founded in 1819, fought against what they perceived to be the negative influence of the industrial north upon the agrarian south. They fought for the preservation of the plantation culture and everything that went with it, including slavery.

Despite hailing from a slaveholding family and state, Clay resisted the rhetoric and found himself drawn instead to the powerful oratory of William Lloyd Garrison, a prominent abolitionist. It became clear to the young Clay that slavery needed to be eliminated but not at the cost of the Union. Clay, like his cousin, the influential Senator Henry Clay, was an emancipationist, fighting for slavery's end through legal and peaceful means. He left school buoyed with optimism for the future.

The abolitionist Cassius Clay haunts the house where he was born and died.

He married Mary Jane Wakefield shortly after his graduation and began to speak out openly against slavery. Clay's ideas threatened an entire way of life and people did oppose his ideas, although he was adamant that violence not be used to end slavery.

His opponents were not nearly as accommodating. In 1843, Samuel Brown, a hired assassin, shot Clay in the chest. Clay responded with his Bowie knife, slicing the ear, nose and cheek of his attacker. Brown's bullet had found its mark but had been stopped by the scabbard Clay always wore across his chest. Clay escaped without injury. In 1849, a mob attacked Clay and while he struggled for his life, he was disarmed. When order was restored, Clay lay unconscious. His breastbone was severed and he had been stabbed in the lung. He survived but needed months to recover fully.

After his recovery, Clay was speaking in public again, this time on behalf of his cousin, Henry, who was hoping to gain the Whig Party's presidential nomination. But when the latter sent a missive to Cassius Clay asking him to relax his rhetoric so as not to offend the Southern Whigs, the letter was intercepted by abolitionists in the north. It was trumpeted in the press as evidence of Henry Clay's Southern sympathies. He lost the nomination.

Cassius Clay continued to promote his views, establishing *The True American* in Lexington in 1845. Death threats were common, and it's said that in his newspaper offices, he kept a pair of loaded cannons, their muzzles pointed towards the front doors, ready to unleash their fearsome brand of deterrence at anyone who dared threaten the newspaper's operation. Despite these precautions, Clay's Lexington offices were overrun, the machinery disassembled and sent north to Cincinnati. Resistance there forced Clay to move his operations once again, this time to Louisville where he changed the paper's name to the *Examiner*.

He worked tirelessly, donating land and money to create a school for non-slaveholders in Kentucky, forming the foundations for what is now Berea College. Speaking tours took him throughout the north. In 1854, he stopped in Springfield, Illinois, where he met a lawyer named Abraham Lincoln. When Lincoln announced his intentions to run for the Republican Party's presidential nomination, Clay threw his support behind him.

When Lincoln ascended to the presidency and began working on the Emancipation Proclamation, he consulted his old friend for advice. Lincoln feared that the proclamation might alienate Kentucky. Clay assured Lincoln that Kentucky had long ago made its stand and the Proclamation would do little to alter allegiances. Weeks later, Lincoln signed the Emancipation Proclamation, an act in which Clay had played no small role. He considered the moment the crowning glory of a life spent fighting for those who had been denied a voice.

In his later years, Clay became more and more withdrawn. Suspicion towards Republican radicalism during Reconstruction led to a split with the party he had helped create; the resulting disillusionment led him to the Democrats. When his health began to deteriorate, Clay retreated to Clermont, his family's home.

Green Clay had built Clermont in 1799, a Georgian-style brick home with seven rooms. When Green Clay died, the home was passed on to his son. Cassius put his own personal stamp on the place in 1860, when architects Thomas Lewinski and John McMurty oversaw Clermont's renovation and expansion. White Hall, as the home is now known, was enlarged to 44 rooms, and ceilings were extended to 16 feet. There was a sweeping staircase running 30 steps, each almost 50 inches wide. The home incorporated technological advances rare for its time: a central heating system and an indoor bathroom.

At the age of 83, Clay remarried, inciting public outrage when people found that he had taken as his wife the 15-year-old daughter of a local farmer, Dora Richardson. Clay, as ever, remained defiant, challenging those who objected to take her from him. Unfortunately for Clay, Richardson left him after only a year of marriage.

White Hall, the mansion Cassius Clay seems reluctant to leave

Clay died alone in White Hall, in the older section of the home, of kidney failure on July 22, 1903. He was buried in Richmond Cemetery, a grand Victorian monument marking his final resting place.

White Hall was passed down through various generations until it was purchased by the state in 1967 at the urging of the governor, Louie B. Nunn. Restored to its original splendor, the home is now a Kentucky Historic Site, paying tribute to one of the state's more colorful political figures and suspected ghosts.

Tourists and Kentuckians go to White Hall every Halloween to see Cassius Clay's life reenacted, as students from Eastern Kentucky act out episodes from Clay's life in what have become called Ghost Walks. Of course, most do not expect the spirit of Clay himself to make an appearance, although he sometimes does. A student writing about her experiences on Lina Linns' *Kentucky Home and Ghost Stories* website volunteered at White Hall for four years. Like others, she had heard the stories about White Hall being haunted, but never lent much credence to the accounts. Ghosts and the paranormal, she thought, were the stuff of fiction. But that was before her volunteer work at the site began.

During her first year there, the student was scheduled to perform in one of the home's outdoor kitchens, but when she went there she found the door locked, and she did not have a key. She turned her back to the door and called out to the nearby director to unlock the door. When she turned back, she gasped. The door was wide open, having been opened by invisible hands. "It brought tears to my eyes," the student wrote.

Her experiences did not end there. That same year, as she was changing in a third-floor room, she noticed flickering candlelight illuminating the dark recesses of the ceiling. Of course, there was no candle in the room. Two years later, the student was in a second-floor room and saw a shadow moving across the floor. She turned to say hello to whoever was passing behind her but found herself staring at an empty room.

While Clay died almost a century ago, it's rumored that he never left the home where he spent so many years and where his life both began and ended. Sightings and reports over the years describe Clay's ghost pacing back and forth through White Hall's windows; people claim he waits there, hoping that someday his ex-wife will return. In the meantime, he is a gracious host, entertaining and assisting the people who continue to visit his house.

Rhode Island
The Sprague Mansion

Rhode Island's historic Sprague family was grand in every way, its manifold accomplishments as august as its failures were tragic. The family's history featured fantastic wealth and power, the laurels of military glory and the arrangement of dynastic marriage, and there are few clans in the history of the United States that can claim comparable successes. But all these lofty achievements were matched by troubles as disastrous as the Sprague family's acquisitions were fortuitous. Premature death among the family's senior members marred the Sprague family account in the 19th century, and political and nuptial scandal made the venerable family into a subject for society gossip. The ultimate deterioration of the family fortune in the 1870s marked the end of the Spragues' tenure as one of the preeminent American families.

While the Spragues' greatness was a thing of the past by the late 1800s, their tortured legacy did not recede so easily. The drama of the wealthy Rhode Island family continues to find voice in the enormous Sprague Mansion that still stands in Cranston, Rhode Island. Once the seat of power for the rich clan, it now serves as the headquarters for the Cranston Historical Society and is also considered one of the most haunted locations of the Ocean State.

The first phase of the Sprague Mansion was constructed in 1790, financed by William Sprague, a local businessman who operated a gristmill on the banks of the Pocasset River. Originally, the house was a humble abode. William himself was pragmatic, more concerned with tending to the family business than with surrounding himself with the trappings of luxury. His attention to finance did not go unrewarded.

Replacing his gristmill with a cotton mill in 1807, William founded the Cranston Print Works, a business that would make the Sprague family one of the giants of the American textile industry. Within a few years, the Spragues became one of the country's biggest calico producers, while paving the way for chemical bleaching of fabric.

But the architect of the Sprague success story would not live to see its ultimate fruition. William died in 1836, after a failed surgical attempt to remove a fishbone he had swallowed. The Cranston Print Works was inherited by William's two able sons, Amasa and William Jr. It was under these two men's stewardship that the Spragues became Rhode Island's most celebrated family. While both brothers were elected to the state legislature, William had more of an affinity for rubbing shoulders and focused most of his attention on politicking. Amasa threw the bulk of his energies into managing the Print Works, just as William, the "boy governor" of Rhode Island, was appointed to the Senate. Yet misfortune was never far behind the Sprague achievements.

On December 31, 1843, Amasa left for Johnston on a business trip; it was a journey he would never complete. His body was found the next day, only a few miles from home, face down in the snow just off the Johnston road, as cold as the frozen red snow that spread around his lifeless limbs. Authorities determined that the textile tycoon had been bludgeoned to death and robbed shortly after he had left the Sprague home the day before. A man named John Gordon became a suspect in the murder and was hanged after he was found guilty during a hasty trial. The tragedy of Amasa's death darkened several shades when evidence emerged that exonerated the man who was executed by the state. It was impossible to bring Gordon back, but the ensuing public furor impelled the state legislature to amend its penal system;

John Gordon was the last convict to be executed in Rhode Island. As for the man who had taken Amasa's life, his identity would never be revealed.

After the death of his brother, William took the reins of the family business. Under him, the Cranston Print Works continued to flourish, with the Sprague fortune reaching its peak in the mid-1860s as the company became the largest calico producer in the world. The 1860s were eventful years for the Sprague heir. William distinguished himself as a brave officer in 1861 when he had his horse shot out from underneath him during the battle of Bull Run. He became known as one of the more ardent Union statesmen, personally financing the formation of Rhode Island regiments. In 1863, he wed Kate Chase, an ambitious Washington socialite who was the daughter of Salmon Chase, Secretary of the Treasury. It is said that William's wedding gift to his young bride was a diamond tiara worth $50,000.

It was also at this time that William took it on himself to renovate the Sprague home in Cranston. Construction began in 1864, transforming the spacious modesty of the original Sprague household into a sprawling Victorian mansion. But there would be little in the way of familial happiness within the lofty walls of the Sprague Mansion. William and Kate were not well suited for each other, and their incessant fighting soon consumed every part of their home life. Things had gotten really bad by the 1870s; William was drinking far too much and began resorting to physical violence during the frequent rows with his wife. When the flagging family business was no longer able to support Kate's excessive spending, not even the strength of Victorian convictions could keep the couple together. The Sprague Mansion was put up for sale, William and Kate divorced and the once powerful Rhode Island family fell into obscurity.

But that is not the end of their story. Today, the tumultuous events of the Sprague family record are interesting not only to local history buffs. Strange accounts began emerging from the Sprague Mansion soon after it was sold. Stories of strange moans drifting down the halls in the middle of the night, of cold spots that move through the dank air of the wine cellar, of invisible forces that throw blankets off sleepers in the middle of the night...it seems as if there is something in Sprague Mansion that refuses to rest, something that continues to brood in the cold opulence of the old manor.

Given the dramatic story of Rhode Island's most famous family, there is no shortage of theories explaining the eerie happenings in the 19th-century home. Some say that the spirit of William Sr. is responsible for these supernatural disturbances. It may be that, obsessed with the downfall of the empire he founded, he is unable or unwilling to leave the Sprague Mansion. Perhaps he is refusing to let go of the one earthly possession he believes should be his family's inalienable right. Certainly such a belief would be in keeping with the proud patriarch's psychology. There are also those who believe that William Sr.'s ghost was responsible for the dissolution of Kate and William Jr.'s marriage, that the constant presence of the elderly Sprague spirit in the house was too much for the distraught couple to deal with.

Others attribute the bizarre phenomena in the mansion to the angry ghost of Amasa Sprague, who was robbed of his life just before the family business became successful. Or perhaps the spirit of John Gordon haunts the home of the man he was falsely convicted of killing; there are a good many paranormal investigators who believe this is the case. Could it be that the ghost who haunts the Sprague Mansion is not even a member of the Sprague family?

While paranormal enthusiasts debate the identity of the haunt in Sprague Mansion, the mysterious entity continues to roam over the sprawling building, which now houses the Cranston Historical Society. Many visitors have witnessed the inexplicable footfalls, flickering lights and cold spots through the mansion; there are some, however, who have actually *seen* an apparition. According to them, the ghost of the Sprague Mansion is a humanoid shape surrounded by thick tendrils of gray mist. The ghost has been spotted all over the mansion, but it seems to be especially attached to the building's main staircase, where it has been seen most often, descending slowly until it dissipates into nothingness at the foot of the stairs.

Reportedly, a séance was once held to determine exactly who was haunting the old house. To everyone's surprise, the séance revealed the presence of a ghost that had no connection to the Spragues at all. According to the medium, the disgruntled spirit summoned was of one of the former owner's butlers. The butler was upset because the owner willed nothing to his long-employed servant. Just as the medium was about to speak the butler's name, the Ouija board suddenly came to life, spelling "My land!" over and over with incredible speed.

For many, the séance resolved nothing, as some speculated that the spirit they reached could have been any mischievous shade—the ghost of one of the Spragues or poor old John Gordon—trying to deceive them. What the séance did confirm was that there is a very strong supernatural presence in the Sprague Mansion. And whatever its reasons for being there, the spirit continues to haunt the old building, giving many visitors to the Cranston Historical Society a dynamic, if somewhat eerie, exposure to Rhode Island's past.

MASSACHUSETTS
The Joshua Ward House

Salem, Massachusetts. If the name of any place in America evokes images of the supernatural, this old New England port town would be the one. Barren trees lining colonial avenues, low clouds hanging over a darkening sky, black cats slinking around foreboding old houses and, of course, the ever-present sense that the specter of a long-dead witch might suddenly appear around the very next corner. In the public eye, every day is Halloween in Salem.

If this is a bit of an exaggeration, it is certainly true that the past weighs heavy on this Massachusetts town. The infamous witch trials of 1692 seem to have burned an indelible mark on the place. And while there are those among us who might scoff at the idea that events of 300 years ago still have the power to frighten, we would do well to respect the force of history, which, time and again, has proven capable of coming back to haunt us. There are none more certain of this than those who have had the misfortune of coming face to face with one of the long-dead specters from Salem's troubled past.

Many people have had such experiences in the town. Some have seen the ghost of an elderly woman in the House of the Seven Gables—the same house where literary great Nathaniel Hawthorne received inspiration to write the horror story by the same name. Others have seen the spirit of what is suspected to be Abigail Ropes in the Ropes Mansion. The Massachusetts grande dame was said to have been standing too close to the fireplace in her bedroom and was quickly engulfed in flames after the fire caught on her nightgown. There are also the stories of the spirit of Giles Corey haunting the Old Jail.

The house that Joshua Ward built is still considered one of the spookiest sites in Salem.

Corey was accused of being a warlock. He refused to go to trial and died after a brutal two-day interrogation where he was crushed to death under stone weights. His apparition has appeared at the Old Jail numerous times since, staring blankly before terrified onlookers. It is said that without fail, some local calamity follows shortly after he appears. Giles Corey isn't the only casualty of 1692 that appears before frightened onlookers. Condemned witches have appeared around Gallows Hill on some evenings, transparent images of women dressed in colonial attire drifting about aimlessly. These female wraiths are also said to be harbingers of calamity to those who see them.

But of all the ghosts in Salem that have their roots in the infamous witch trials of 1692, the most talked about would be the spirit that drifts through the Joshua Ward House. The mansion, a three-story brownstone, was built in the late 1700s by one of Salem's premier merchants, Joshua Ward. It was built on Salem Harbor, with a view of the water that brought in Mr. Ward's cargo-laden ships from abroad. By all accounts, nothing too out of the ordinary transpired in the mansion while Joshua Ward lived in it. He was an esteemed member of the Salem gentry, and it is entirely possible that the master of the house made sure his servants kept quiet about home life in the Ward House to avert unwanted whispering. For almost everyone who has lived in the house since the original owner passed on has come away with thoughts of the afterlife foremost in their minds.

Those seeking explanations for the bizarre events occurring in the Joshua Ward House have been drawn to the very foundations the house was built upon, to the wooden house that once stood where the brick mansion stands today. George Corwin, Sheriff of Essex County, resided in the house during the Salem witch trials. One of the judges of the controversial proceedings that sent 19 people to the scaffold and saw more than 100 New Englanders jailed, Corwin was also in charge of all property confiscated from convicted witches. It was said that he made a small fortune selling the lands of these unfortunates, growing ever wealthier as the grisly witch hunts continued.

Corwin's role in the 1692 trials did not make him popular in Salem, and after the witch hysteria died away, the innumerable silent accusations whispered over the succeeding years reshaped his identity within the community, changing him from a respected judge into an accomplice in murder. None hated Corwin more than Bob and Mary English, a couple accused of witchcraft who fled to New York before they could be brought to trial. Returning to Massachusetts after the hysteria died down, the Englishes discovered that George Corwin, acting on behalf of the state, had sold their estate. They tried suing to get their property back, but the court of law at the time forbade any legal action against the county government.

Yet local lore tells us that Bob and Mary were able to win one grisly prize in their legal wrangling with Essex Count. Legend has it that the Salem court, in a bizarre twist of colonial legality, awarded the Englishes a lien on George Corwin's corpse. While it was a worthless prize, it was the only compensation the couple were given for their losses, and they clung to it with the kind of fervor reserved for the most profoundly wronged. When Corwin died, it was said Bob and Mary waited outside his house, promising they would seize the former sheriff's corpse the moment it was removed from his house. The Corwin family, disgusted by the morbid determination of the Englishes, were determined to keep Corwin's remains in the family and buried George in the cellar floor.

A dead person entombed within a house is almost a surefire way to acquire a haunting. But it did not end there. Seventeen years after Corwin was buried in the basement, his remains were disinterred to receive a proper burial in one of the local cemeteries. Joshua Ward had the Corwin home demolished to build his own mansion on the site.

Oddly enough, the Ward House haunting doesn't seem to be perpetrated solely by the spirit of George Corwin. In fact, the most distinguishable ghost in the house isn't the old

Essex County sheriff, but an anonymous woman whose apparition has begun to appear with increased frequency over the last decade.

Richard Carlson purchased the Ward House in the late 1900s, intending to make the building the headquarters for his realty company, Carlson Realty. He had no way of knowing that the house he had bought was unlike any piece of real estate he had ever bought or sold before. The first indicator that things in the house were not as they seemed came from a house alarm that seemed to operate with a will of its own, sounding in the middle of the night for no reason at all. It became a regular chore for Richard Carlson or his partner, Julie Tache, to get out of bed and shut the alarm off. It happened so often that the couple began to notice that whoever was operating the alarm seemed to prefer Richard to Julie. For while the alarm would shut off the moment Richard opened the front door and stepped inside, when Julie went out to turn the system off she would have to go all the way down to the cellar before the alarm quit. Who was triggering the alarm, and how did it seemingly shut off by itself? Difficult questions, which Julie and Richard tried to ignore as best they could.

Other individuals have had far more vivid experiences in the Joshua Ward House. One of Carlson Realty's clients was in her real estate agent's office in the middle of a busy afternoon when their business was interrupted by the agent's telephone. The woman was waiting for the realtor to get off the telephone when her eyes fell on a sight that made the hairs on the back of her neck bristle instinctively. Sitting in an enormous wing chair against one wall of the hallway was a haggard-looking woman.

Her alabaster skin was slightly translucent, so that the wall was faintly discernable behind her. Her jet black hair was a wild mess of madcap tangles, and she was dressed in anachronistic clothing the likes of which the real estate client had never seen before. People walked up and down the hallway, oblivious to the lone woman sitting there, staring blankly ahead with an expressionless look on her face. When her realtor got off the telephone, the disturbed client promptly asked who the woman in the hallway was, only to receive a curt reply: "What woman?"

Turning her gaze back to the hallway, the stunned client was unable to offer any response as she took stock of the now-empty chair. Before she left the building, she asked a number of other employees if they had seen the lady sitting in the wingback earlier on, but not a single person had. One realtor who had a clear line of sight from behind his desk to the hallway chair swore that nobody had sat in the wingback chair all day. The shaken client left the Ward House that day, determined never to return.

Another individual who developed an aversion to the old building was the real estate company's custodian. The man would clean the office in the early evening after everyone had gone home. He had never felt comfortable in the house by himself and went through his duties as quickly as possible, spending no more time there than necessary. But he altered his work habits after one evening when an invisible hand reached out of the darkness to grab his elbow as he climbed the first-floor stairs. When the man spun around to face whoever had grabbed him, he found himself staring into empty space. Not one minute later, the janitor was out the door and in his car, shaking in fear. He stopped working evenings in the Ward House after that, choosing instead to come in during the morning, when the office staff were starting their day.

Shortly after the custodian changed his hours, employees of Carlson Realty were treated to another bizarre event. The

Joshua Ward House, where various residents have been shocked by the apparition of a pale woman with crazy hair.

realtors were posing for staff photos outside the building when one of the Ward House's invisible inhabitants made an unexpected appearance. She showed up in a Polaroid taken of a Carlson employee. In lieu of a well-dressed real estate agent was a woman with crazy black hair and pale skin, dressed in ragged 17th-century clothing, looking blankly at the camera.

This mysterious spirit grew bolder after the real estate office moved out of the Joshua Ward House. The people who worked for the small publishing company that occupied the brick building after Carlson Realty had flexible arrangements with their employer, coming into the office whenever they were able. The spirit must have felt more comfortable appearing before smaller audiences, because over the next few years, numerous people caught a glimpse of the same pale apparition while working alone in the office. One editor caught sight of the woman early one morning and saw the apparition slowly walk down the first-floor stairs before fading into nothingness.

A local band given permission to practice in the Ward House basement probably had the most dramatic encounter with the pale lady. Permitted to play only when no one was in the building working, the band was in the middle of a song when the drummer looked up to see the woman with scraggly black hair silently staring at the musicians. By this time, the apparition had become something of a local legend. The drummer knew that he was staring at an object that was not of this world—and he was scared. "Everyone get out, now!" he yelled at his surprised band mates, who couldn't see anything besides each other. After running out to the parking lot behind the building, the band listened to the drummer explain what he had just seen when a freakish moan drifted up from the basement speakers, a sound that suddenly made everyone in the parking lot freezing cold. The woman was wailing through one of the band's microphones, using the speakers to express some profound and ageless misery. The band never practiced in the Ward House basement again.

To this day, the identity of the pale apparition is a mystery. After all, it was George Corwin's remains that were buried in the foundations of the Joshua Ward House, so shouldn't it be his likeness that appears to frightened onlookers today? Perhaps the woman is one of the witches George Corwin passed judgment on, and her soul, unable to rest, haunts the closest thing on earth to the corrupt colonial magistrate: the foundations of his former home. And maybe not.

Some have speculated that strange things have always been afoot in Salem, and that it was such inexplicable occurrences that led to the witch trials of 1692, more than any personal rivalries, adolescent mischief or plain malevolence. These people might suggest that there actually *were* witches in Salem three centuries ago, and the power of their magic there was very real. As they are with all other hauntings, any explanations are loaded with uncertainty. A gray area that the Salem witches continue to occupy in the American consciousness, celebrated every year at the end of October, when the leaves turn orange, the days go dark and the cold bite of winter comes riding in on the wind.

MISSISSIPPI
McRaven House

In Vicksburg, one house is haunted by a Civil War spirit who reflects the turbulent history of the city. Founded in 1811 along the mighty Mississippi River, Vicksburg grew rapidly as a center for commerce, agriculture and river traffic. In 1831, with the completion of the Vicksburg-Clinton railroad line, the city had become the western link of the only east-west railroad between Memphis and New Orleans. Looking down the Mississippi from its perch high on the bluffs, the city gained a reputation during the Civil War as the Gibraltar of the Confederacy, the key to the South's defense of the river. As long as the Mississippi remained under Southern control, the South could remain whole. The North recognized this fact and launched a campaign to wrest control of the river from the South.

By 1863, Vicksburg was the last of the great Mississippi River port cities left under Confederate control. New Orleans, Baton Rouge and Natchez had already fallen. The Northern campaign for Vicksburg began in earnest in the spring. The Union General Ulysses S. Grant attacked the fortress city but was repelled. He realized that it could not be taken directly; instead, he would suffocate the city. He established a line of works around Vicksburg, successfully severing the city from supplies and outside communication. For the next 47 days, Grant placed the city under a constant barrage of cannon fire. Soldier and citizen alike suffered during the siege and many began carving caves out of the hillsides to escape the artillery fire. With supplies dwindling, Vicksburg residents grew desperate for food. Surrender suddenly became a viable option.

On July 4, 1863, Vicksburg fell. The Union had now in its grasp the last remaining Southern stronghold along the

Mississippi. With the defeat, the Confederacy was decisively split in two. Vicksburg chose to remember its defeat by refusing to celebrate the Fourth of July for 81 years. Grant's victory, combined with Meade's bloody stand at Gettysburg, turned the tide of the Civil War.

Union troops occupied Vicksburg and they made their headquarters in the McRaven House. Colonel Wilson was left in command. To ease the occupation of a city embittered by the horrors of siege and destruction, he turned to Captain McPherson, a former resident. Nightly, McPherson would make rounds around town, listening to the complaints of the people and the roughly 30,000 paroled Confederate soldiers. One fateful evening, McPherson failed to return from his tour.

Ill will towards the Union in Vicksburg ran strong, and memories of death and suffering did not fade quickly. Wilson realized as much when, sitting in McRaven House, he looked up to see the bloodied and mutilated apparition of his missing captain, soaking wet. He told his commander that he had been murdered by Confederate sympathizers and thrown into the river. Ever since his disappearance, residents of McRaven House from Colonel Wilson to its current occupant, Leyland French, have been treated to the sight of the murdered captain wandering the halls in silent testament to the house's particularly tortured history.

Built in 1797, McRaven House served as a field hospital during the siege of Vicksburg and was even witness to a battle in its backyard. It's not surprising that a multitude of lost spirits continues to wander the grounds, giving McRaven House its reputation as the most haunted home in Mississippi. No one knows exactly how many spirits are still around, but it is believed that at least five of the home's owners died in or around the house. Moreover, many of those who died while it served as a field hospital are buried on its grounds. The ghosts are friendly but they hearken back to darker times when the soul of the United States was cleaved in two and brother fought against brother. Even after the Civil War ended, its legacy left an indelible mark on Vicksburg through the bankruptcy and the internal strife of the reconstruction governments. Today's Vicksburg is a community of 30,000 whose role in the war is memorialized by both a national park and the ghosts of McRaven House.

WASHINGTON, D.C.
Octagon Mansion

Before the completion of the President's House in Washington, D.C., another home rose from the swamps to become the first residence in the city. For the city's planners, among them George Washington and Pierre Charles L'Enfant, this first house represented the formalization of what had been, until then, just plans on a page. The Octagon Mansion represented the concrete embodiment of an abstract vision. The countryside would soon be transformed into a collection of streets, avenues, homes and parks, the embodiment of Washington's vision for a Federal City.

William Thornton, the architect responsible for the Capitol Building, designed this first home, named the Octagon Mansion for unknown reasons (it has only six sides, not eight), for a close friend of George Washington's, Colonel John Tayloe III. Tayloe, at the time, was the wealthiest of the Virginian plantation owners, and Washington encouraged him to build his winter home in the nation's capital. Tayloe bought his plot of land at what would be the corner of 18th Street and New York Avenue in 1799 and construction began

Tumultuous events left their paranormal imprint on the remarkable Octagon Mansion.

immediately. Because of L'Enfant's street plans, 18th and New York created an oddly shaped lot that necessitated the singularly unique design of the Octagon.

Thornton conceived of a three-story brick house that would represent a dramatic break from the Georgian style, the dominant design of the time. His plan combined a circle, two rectangles and a triangle, resulting in the home's six sides and a grand example of the Federal style. The home was completed in 1801, made of locally produced bricks, timber, iron and sandstone, while decorative elements and furniture had been shipped from England.

Tayloe, his wife Ann Ogle, seven sons and eight daughters first lived there in 1801, spending winters there until 1817 when they decided that it would make a fine year-round residence. By then, the Octagon was already one of the most famous buildings in a capital replete with monuments. In 1814, when the British torched the President's House, James and Dolly Madison moved into the Octagon before moving back into what would forever after be known as the White House. The Treaty of Ghent, bringing peace between Britain and the United States, was signed in the Octagon's second-floor parlor on February 17, 1815. Both the Madisons and Tayloes loved entertaining and many of Washington's elite passed in and out of the Octagon, marveling at its grand rotunda and sweeping oval staircase. Within years, the Octagon had become the centerpiece on a street lined with grand and magnificent mansions. Sadly, Tayloe never felt the same way about his grand home; instead, the Octagon, through family strife and tragedy, became the embodiment of pain, sorrow and loss.

Tayloe was a man of strong principles and while he allowed the import of British goods for use in the decoration of his home, he refused, at any social level, to associate with a Briton. Years of war with England in both the American Revolution and the War of 1812 had hardened his disdain for America's former imperial master. It's not surprising, then, that when his daughter fell in love with a British officer, the stage was set for a tragedy of Shakespearean proportions.

Despite all his daughter's protests, Tayloe refused to bend to her requests. Passions ran high on both sides, as Tayloe did what he thought was his best to protect his daughter from committing a grave error, while his daughter, her determination fortified by love, would not relent in her quest to marry the man of her choice. No resolution ever emerged from the frequent arguments. The affair came to its end when, one night, after another fierce discussion, the daughter grabbed her candle and ran up the stairs. As she neared the summit, she shrieked. She slipped on the stairs and tumbled to her death.

Tayloe was devastated by the loss, but the death had little effect on his stubborn nature, and it wasn't long before he found himself in a similar position with another daughter, one who eloped, rejecting the suitor her father had chosen for her. She returned to the Octagon to beg her father's forgiveness. They met on the stairs but Tayloe refused to listen. Instead, he pushed past his daughter and continued on down the stairs. The girl lost her balance, falling past her father down the stairs to her death.

Tayloe had never quite recovered from the shock of losing his first daughter and, having witnessed the death of another under eerily similar circumstances, his spirit was crippled, the losses plunging him into a depression from which he would never recover. The strain was more than his already fragile constitution could bear, and Tayloe died shortly after at 57, in 1828, having spent the last few years of his life avoiding the Octagon as much as possible.

After her husband's death, Ann Ogle lived in the Octagon until she died in 1855, at which point the home changed hands a number of times and became, towards the latter part of the 19th century, a tenement packed with renters. It seemed that few wanted to hold onto the Octagon for long despite its prestigious pedigree. Many were scared because they swore the place was haunted, as described in newspaper reports dating from the 19th century. Indeed, during the waning days of the Civil War, the Octagon was used as both a records office and a hospital. Many a soldier met his maker in the halls of the Octagon, so it's not surprising that residents would hear unearthly screams, sobs and moans echoing through the Octagon. Ghostly echoes of Tayloe's daughters' deaths were also heard. More than one tenant claimed to see a candle wending its way up the oval staircase, only to tumble down the stairs, at which point a sickening thud

The ghostly echoes of two fatal falls are heard in a stairwell in the Octagon Mansion.

would echo through the rotunda. In 1891, the Catholic organization Sisters of Charity took possession of the home but left soon after. Even after the house was purified and blessed with holy water, the ghosts refused to leave. Although Tayloe was happy to be rid of the Octagon, Dolly Madison, who lived in the home for only a year, never forgot the place. Her ghost has been seen near the second-floor fireplace, always accompanied by the scent of lilacs.

The Octagon Mansion finally found a permanent owner in 1902, when the American Institute of Architects bought the home. During renovations, workmen were puzzled by the repeated knocking they heard by one particular section of wall. They tore into the wall and discovered the skeletal remains of a young woman. The remains were buried and from that time on, the hallway has remained silent. The other ghosts, however, continue to make their presence felt. Chandeliers on the main floor swing and the phantom shrieks of Tayloe's daughters and the rattling of Civil War sabers are heard. In 1996, extensive work was done to restore the Octagon to its original condition, fitting for a home in which the past continues to exert its influence.

MARYLAND
Cellar House Plantation

On 60 acres of plush Maryland landscape, Cellar House Plantation is the very picture of American pastoralism. In a world away from the chaotic rush of the country's metropolises, the life that teems around the old Cellar House is mostly local fauna. There, one is more likely to spot a bounding deer, creeping woodland vole or darting hare than an American citizen. Cellar House sits on a ridge overlooking the Pocomoke River, about a mile south of Milburn Landing State Park. The stately 18th-century home was purchased by a Salisbury architect named John Graham in the 1960s and has been a home for the Graham family ever since.

Mr. Graham knew that he wasn't purchasing typical real estate when he bought the Cellar House estate. The site of one of Maryland's most infamous murders, the house on the river is surrounded by gore and mystery. It is the focal point of one the state's most enduring folk tales—a story that features nuptial infidelity, a family torn asunder and a violent crime of homicidal passion.

Cellar House dates back to the 1740s, but it rests on foundations that go back further than that, to a 1666 land grant bestowed on a French sea captain by Lord Baltimore. This French captain built the house on the Pocomoke shortly after he took a bride, furnishing the home with luxuries that were rarely found on the austere east coast settlements of that time. We have no way of knowing how well the couple got along, but it is said that the captain soon came under financial difficulty and began smuggling illegal goods as a way to make ends meet.

He dug a secret tunnel from the river's edge to the cellar of his home, where he would store all the contraband he smuggled in from abroad. Rumors began to spread about the wealth in the captain's cellar, and locals were soon referring to the place as Cellar House, whispering about the untold wealth that was stored underneath the captain's home. To this day, some people believe there may be treasures buried somewhere on Cellar House Plantation, an inheritance that no descendants lived long enough to claim for their own. For despite the massive wealth that the captain was said to amass in his cellar, his family would become legendary in its violent demise.

Sailing great distances, the captain was absent from home for long stretches of time, leaving behind a lonely wife who often spent months in isolation. Desperate for company, the young woman eventually took notice of a seafarer who sailed his vessel up and down the Pocomoke regularly. Their relationship began innocently, with the young sailor stopping off at the wharf for dinner, but their loneliness was a potent catalyst to their mutual attraction, and it wasn't long before the two were embroiled in an adulterous affair.

They managed to keep it from the French seaman for quite some time, even after the woman gave birth to a child that she believed was fathered by her lover rather than her husband. But her devious arrangement did not last forever. The ill-fated evening was a moonless one, when the French sea captain, weary from months of travel on the stormy Atlantic, piloted his ship up the Pocomoke only to see that another ship was docked at his wharf. All of his worst suspicions were confirmed when the captain stormed into his bedchamber to find his wife under the sheets with another man.

The woman's paramour just managed to get out of the house with his life that night, but the unfortunate woman would never greet another dawn with a smile. After suffering a terrible beating at the hands of her husband, she, along with her infant, was banished from the house. But the dishonored woman had nowhere to go and no means to provide even the most basic shelter. Days later, with a starving child in her arms and despair in her heart, the estranged woman turned her eyes back to her husband's door, hoping to win forgiveness.

Disaster struck before she even reached home. It was a stormy night when the woman began her journey back to Cellar House, and the vessel she was in overturned in the Pocomoke's rushing waters; she lost her child in her frantic swim to the river's edge. The screams of her terrified drowning infant were ringing in her ears as she trudged through the surrounding swampland, so that the grief-ridden woman was half mad by the time she showed up at Cellar House's front door. But the Frenchman, having spent weeks festering in a drunken malaise, was nowhere near a state of forgiveness, and when the source of his misery showed up on his doorstep he flew into a murderous rage. Dragging the poor woman up to the same room where he had witnessed her tryst, he ended her tortured life with a knife in the chest, leaving her to die on the bedroom floor.

It is said that the Frenchman set sails to his ship that night and floated down the Pocomoke to the Atlantic Ocean, never to return to Maryland again. The woman's body was discovered weeks later, rotting on the bedroom floor where she had fallen. Cellar House was left unoccupied for years, as the weeds on the grounds grew as tall as the tales about the tragic events that had transpired during the building's first years.

There was good reason the story stayed alive. On stormy summer nights, locals have heard eerie sounds coming off the river. Amid torrential rain and crashing thunder, the fragile wail of a terrified child travels on the wind, waking some of the people who live on the banks of the Pocomoke. Those in deep slumber often sleep through the child's timid cries, only to be woken by the horrible scream that is said to always follow. This cry is a spine-tingling sound, tortured and prolonged, drifting in from the darkness of the blustering night. Others have heard strange sounds from Cellar House itself—the fearful cries of a desperate woman in mortal danger, the roaring response of a man possessed by terrible intentions.

These occurrences have been repeatedly documented over succeeding generations, with neighbors, campers and boaters reporting bizarre sounds coming from Cellar House at odd hours. While such accounts have secured Cellar House's place in Maryland's tome of supernatural folklore, residents of the old home have surprisingly been able to enjoy the bucolic luxury of Cellar House Plantation. Though it has been left deserted for decades at a time during its history, affluent Marylanders have always come back to the house on the Pocomoke.

In 1966, John Graham found disturbing evidence that there might be something behind the legends. For while he was supervising the renovations to the old house, his crew unearthed a skeleton in the house cellar, buried in the dirt ground of the 300-year-old subterranean storage room. Fearing that it might be the remains of the adulterous woman, Mr. Graham had two archeologists study the corpse. The archeologists weren't absolutely certain, but they believed that the skeleton actually was that of an American Indian. Further study of the site suggested that Cellar House might have been built atop an ancient Indian burial ground.

This wasn't comforting news for John Graham, who was growing attached to the house he had just purchased. Yet years have passed, and the Graham family still lives in the historic home, enjoying the splendid comfort and scenery of rural Maryland. Perhaps the ghosts of Cellar House have finally resolved their age-old marital dispute and abandoned their earthly grievances for a peaceful oblivion. Perhaps they have been inspired by the show of general familial content that the Grahams have brought to the area and are no longer locked in their destructive vortex of rage and desperation. Or maybe they simply lie dormant, waiting for an unknown signal to bring them back. It may simply be a matter of time before the horrifying nocturnal howls drift over the Pocomoke's banks once again, terrorizing those who reside in the peaceful plantation.

2
Phantoms in Public

California
The Ghosts of Alcatraz

Few sights are more impressive than the northern approach into San Francisco. The looming towers of the Golden Gate Bridge suddenly rise over Highway 101—orange giants spanning the watery gap that divides San Francisco Bay from the Pacific Ocean. From the famous Fisherman's Wharf teeming with tourists to the frenetic bustle of Union Square, the city is a glittering symbol of the spirit of American enterprise, of what good can be made from the collective will to succeed.

Yet cradled within the heart of the golden city is a dismal reminder of what happens to those disenfranchised unfortunates who run afoul of American society, of those poor and often malicious souls who cannot, or will not, live by the laws of the land. It is Alcatraz, the crumbling and abandoned prison that juts out of San Francisco Bay underneath the storied bridge. Even today, long after the last criminal did his time in the utter isolation of the infamous jail, one can sense an undeniable foreboding emanating from Alcatraz Island.

People felt this apprehension about "the Rock" long before it was designated a federal prison. Long ago, well before San Francisco was founded, the first Miwok Indians who cast their eyes on the small island decided to steer clear of it, feeling that the pelican-covered rock was evil. If the prehistoric account includes no events that corroborated the Miwok premonitions, Alcatraz's eventual role as America's most notorious prison would justify these early Indians' ancient fears.

From 1934 until 1963, some of the most hardened criminals in the United States served time in the renovated maximum-security prison. The walls of "Hellcatraz," as it was called by inmates, were impenetrable, and even if resourceful convicts were able to get through prison security, the cold, choppy waters of the bay provided a final, virtually insurmountable barrier. And while incarceration is a difficult ordeal wherever a prison might be located, the fact that many inmates had windows that opened onto the glittering lights of vivacious San Francisco made imprisonment even worse.

Only the hardest men did time on the Rock. Among their number were killers such as "Machine Gun" Kelly, "Creepy" Karpis, Doc Barker, Abie "Butcher" Maldowitz and one of the most famous crooks of all time, Al Capone. One might expect that a place with such an iniquitous roster of personalities would somehow be affected. Given the testament of so many who have set foot on Alcatraz Island and walked through what is now one of San Francisco's most visited tourist attractions, the incarcerated villains seem to have left some part of themselves behind.

While many visitors have experienced a strong sense that there is more on the island than meets the eye, these feelings have rarely been positive. If supernatural phenomena truly are at work on the forlorn rock, they are not the sorts of occurrences that a person would want to experience alone. From the bloodcurdling screams that have been heard late at night to the sudden crashing sounds that startle visitors in broad daylight, every inexplicable event is tinged with an energy that can only be called sinister.

Different psychics who have visited the island have sensed the spirits of different inmates, many of whom retain their vicious intentions. The spirit of "Butcher" Maldowitz, for example, was felt in a cellblock beset by frequent reports of mysterious footsteps and harsh whispers that seemed to come from nowhere. The psychics who identified the spirit of the

Butcher sensed that he bears no goodwill for those sightseers who casually walk through his own personal hell, and he does everything he can to keep people away. Maldowitz never made it out of Alcatraz; he was killed by a fellow inmate during a jailhouse brawl.

Above the sounds of lapping water, seagulls and visitors, some have heard the faint strains of a banjo drifting through the prison. It has been suggested that this music is performed by Al Capone, the legendary prohibition gangster who served time in Alcatraz for tax evasion. It is difficult to imagine the disappointment Capone must have felt when he was dethroned from his criminal empire. His sudden fall into Alcatraz made him into a common hood whose criminal fame didn't get him an iota of special treatment from the prison's stern warden, James A. Johnston. Perhaps Capone continues to pluck away at his banjo, unable to get over the unforeseen sorrow of his final days.

And then there is the "D" Block. In what is still considered the most haunted area in Alcatraz, horrendous tortures committed against inmates are relived. Used for solitary confinement, the block was reserved for the punishment of inmates who had transgressed jailhouse rules. Cells 9–14 were individually referred to as "the Hole" because they had neither windows nor beds and the one light bulb in the room was usually kept off. Legend has it that one convict cast into the Hole was found dead in his cell a few days later, killed by some mysterious predator unknown to prison guards or fellow inmates.

Today, these cells are almost always colder than the rest of the prison. Eerie wails originate in this area. More than a few visitors have run screaming from the cellblock after feeling a pair of ice-cold hands closing around their throats.

Every year, Alcatraz receives thousands of visitors interested in seeing the legendary prison firsthand. If they're lucky enough, they might even have a supernatural experience with one of the prison's many ghosts. Meanwhile, the surrounding bay and city of San Francisco continue to shine, somehow ignoring the lonely crag and its haunted past.

NEW YORK
The Spirits of St. Mark's

St. Mark's Church in-the-Bowery is tucked away in Manhattan's Lower East Side, a pillar of spiritual propriety standing tall in the scurrying capitalism of modern Manhattan. The church is active within the community. Fostering programs that tend to the welfare of its neighborhood and parish, St. Mark's still manages, in its serene austerity, to stand apart from the hectic bustle of the Big Apple. And it's old—very old. Celebrating its 200th year in 1999, the Episcopal church, with its regal architecture, flourishing arts scene and faithful congregation, is more than an eminent place of worship; it is also one of New York City's oldest historical landmarks.

Since 1799, the church has operated from within the thriving city's heart, serving as an administrative center for philanthropic projects as New York surged through one growing pain after another. At different times over the years, St. Mark's has provided schooling for underprivileged children; served as a meeting place for humanitarian societies; and in the 20th century, has been a respectable venue for local drama—all the while providing its Sunday services to New Yorkers.

But the church's roots run deeper yet into the city's foundations, stretching back to a time when New York was New Amsterdam, the Lower East Side was open farmland and most

St. Mark's Church in-the-Bowery is an important—and haunted—part of New York history.

of the city's inhabitants spoke Dutch. It was 1660 when New York's first governor, Peter Stuyvesant, built a Dutch Reform chapel on the site where St. Mark's stands today. Stuyvesant owned the surrounding land, a sprawling plantation—or "bowery" in Dutch—located just north of New Amsterdam.

Stuyvesant was a haughty Dutch aristocrat, whose drive to achieve worldly wealth overshadowed every other aspect of his character. Many of his contemporaries would probably say that his physical appearance reflected something of his personal priorities. Dressed resplendently in 17th-century Dutch finery, Stuyvesant went about his daily business on the colony, lurching through the streets of New Amsterdam with a cruel fire burning beneath his hard eyes and a hideously misshapen gait. He lost one leg while serving in the military years before, and his wooden peg leg, ostentatiously studded with silver bands, thumped and scraped across the ground wherever he went. The difficult Dutch patriarch ruled the area with a vicious arrogance, so that when the New Englanders of Long Island moved in to occupy New Amsterdam in 1664, the residents welcomed a change in leadership and not a single shot was fired in defense.

Stuyvesant stayed on in the colony after he was deposed, entrenching himself in the opulence of his plantation for eight more years, until death claimed him in 1672. He was buried underneath his chapel, within the vault he requested for his own remains, the first of a long line of Stuyvesants who would be entombed in these catacombs. Though the chapel was eventually torn down, with St. Mark's being erected in its place in 1799, the Stuyvesant vaults remained intact, and members of the Dutch clan continued to be buried there until the 1950s, when the catacombs were finally sealed. Today, it is estimated that there are about 70 coffins laid underneath St. Mark's—saying nothing of the bodies buried in the nearby cemetery that is currently looked after by the Episcopal church.

Today, St. Mark's in-the-Bowery is something of a Janus on the Manhattan cityscape. On the one hand, the church has taken a progressive, proactive stance in the community. Buoyed by a social activism that left its mark on the local clergy in the 1960s, St. Mark's has become deeply involved in local arts while sponsoring numerous programs aimed to improve the urban quality of life.

On the other hand, St. Mark's stands amid one of the oldest burial grounds in New York City. Ever since Peter Stuyvesant was buried there in 1672, corpses have been slowly gathering over the years, and a large cemetery has grown around the church. Like the vaults under St. Mark's, the burial plots in the cemetery are catacombs, large subterranean rooms marked by stone slabs above ground. For those visitors inclined to imagine it, the idea of these underground caverns yawning just underneath the surface has cast St. Mark's in darker, more mysterious, shades.

So it is that as the parish works to foster and celebrate urban life, others perceive the church itself as a monument to the dead. And not an entirely inert monument either. Many of those who have experienced the darker side of St. Mark's have walked away with an acute realization that not all the dead lie still or are irretrievably banished to the past—that some residents of the underworld are intent on remaining in the land of the living.

Given Peter Stuyvesant's obsession with worldly interests—his practically religious pursuit of money, power and prestige—can it be any surprise that his soul is determined to remain on the lands he claimed as his own so many years ago? For it is the spirit of New York's first governor that everyone thinks of whenever another bizarre event transpires at St. Mark's. And not without good reason.

In fact, people around the church have been having bizarre encounters with Stuyvesant for over two centuries now, beginning shortly after the former Dutch aristocrat passed on. More than one housemaid ran screaming from Stuyvesant's property in the middle of the night, crying out that their master had come back from the dead. One popularized account has a sexton who was looking after St. Mark's during the Civil War woken from his sleep by a measured thudding noise in the hall. The sound continued as the man lay in bed, drawing nearer in a slow cadence, until the nocturnal visitor seemed mere yards from the sexton's door. Trembling in fear, the church's steward got up and opened the portal, only to find a deserted hallway.

On another evening shortly after, the caretaker heard the wooden clunking again, but this time when he stepped out of his room to investigate, his eyes corroborated what his ears had heard, though he was anything but happy about it. Lumbering down the hall towards him was none other than Peter Stuyvesant, moving as quickly as he could in an awkward peg-legged locomotion. The sexton reeled back in horror, staring at what may as well have been Stuyvesant's statue come to life. Fleeing from St. Mark's that night, he never returned to the church again.

Others have reported strange sounds coming from the church during the evening hours. For a while in the late 1800s, the bells of St. Mark's acquired an eerie tendency to ring on their own. The bells would suddenly start chiming in the middle of the night, waking everyone in the surrounding neighborhood. More than once, people got up to investigate, but no one was ever found in the church during these forays, even though the bells would still be swaying by the time local residents got to the tower.

While people's experiences in the church have not been as dramatic in recent years, strange occurrences have been consistently reported. Almost invariably, these events take place after the sun has set on Manhattan. Pedestrians passing by the churchyard at night have heard that peg-legged gait which can only be attributed to Peter Stuyvesant. Others have seen faint outlines moving through the darkness of the cemetery, while some swear that a shadow emerged from the darkness of the churchyard, a silhouette somehow darker than the blackness around it, before fading back into the nothingness it came from. And then there are the accounts of whispering, labored breathing and of course the same *thud, thud, thud* that has been heard by more than one petrified passerby through the course of New York's history.

By these accounts, it seems all too apparent that Peter Stuyvesant, in one form or another, continues to inhabit Manhattan. The city today would be completely unrecognizable to the statesman who governed New Amsterdam in the 17th century. But the avaricious Dutchman would hardly be put off by the impressive dimensions of New York today, and perhaps the spirit of Stuyvesant, enthralled by the magnificent wealth of Manhattan, feels more at home in New York today than he ever did when he ruled over it.

COLORADO
Cheesman Park

Disturbing the dead is just not prudent. One might think that would be clear, but there are times when the greatest mysteries are found not in the cosmos or in the ether or in that shadow world between life and death, but among the living. Why do people do the things that they do? What compels them to act without consideration or respect? When faced with the disturbing and uncomfortable, curiosity longs for an answer. Sometimes, human nature refuses to provide one. And then, sometimes, it does, with a truth that is almost as unbearable as ignorance in its embrace of human frailty.

Cheesman Park is an oasis amid a neighborhood of historic grand manors, tidy gardens, sweeping blocks of apartments and towering condominiums. Within its 120 acres are a Greek pavilion, a botanical garden and Congress Park. It is a place that embraces those from all walks of life, whether they are the wealthy elite or the struggling artist or the young professional, a far cry from the prevailing attitudes that dominated during the park's inception.

Cheesman Park was once a cemetery. The story began in 1858 when General William Larimer claimed 120 acres east of the newly founded settlement of Denver. His goal was to set a cemetery in a glorious park-like setting, but a lack of water meant that his vision would not be realized. He soldiered on, though, and Mount Prospect Graveyard accepted its first two residents in March 1860—Jack O'Neal, a gambler, and John Skoetal, his killer. A segregated cemetery, Mount Prospect had plots and areas set aside for the wealthy, Catholics and minorities.

Problems arose when challenges were made to Larimer's land titles; settlers seeking land for their homesteads and undertaker John J. Walley all laid claims. Mount Prospect Cemetery found itself mired in the dispute for years. The case came to the attention of the U.S. Land Office, which ended the issue when it declared the land federal property, nullifying any previous titles. Two years later, in 1872, the land was sold to the city at $1.25 an acre under the stipulation that the land stay a burial ground. Mount Prospect was rechristened as the far more pedestrian and accessible City Cemetery, mirroring Denver's intentions for its new acquisition. It would no longer be the domain of the respectable members of society, but of the downtrodden and the prosecuted—transients, epidemic victims and criminals. The grounds were allowed to fall into a less than pristine state.

With Denver's rapid expansion, demand for land grew, and nowhere was it stronger than in the area of City Cemetery. Rail and mining barons wanted this land for themselves so they could construct their grand mansions in the shadows of the Rocky Mountains. The city was more than willing to oblige. A new cemetery had been built off the banks of the Platte River, and friends and families of the deceased were moving many of the bodies from City Cemetery to plots in the new cemetery.

In 1893, Denver lobbied Congress to designate City Cemetery as park land. The request was approved, and a section of the land was named Congress Park to honor the decision. But Denver now faced a problem. Many of those buried in City Cemetery had no relations or friends to look after the transport of their remains to new plots elsewhere. The city hired an undertaker, Edward McGovern, to move the estimated 5000 bodies.

McGovern was far from scrupulous; he respected neither the dead nor their right to rest in peace. Graves were looted. Determined to cut costs, McGovern and his workers would pack two to three bodies into a single pine coffin. If there wasn't room, corpses were broken up, limbs and appendages lopped off freely so they could fit in the coffins. When McGovern and his men tired of digging up bodies, they filled the coffins with rocks instead of bodies. Since few had mourned their passing, McGovern reasoned, who would stand for the dead now? But McGovern had not counted on the court of public opinion. Local newspapers discovered, quite easily, what he had been doing. McGovern made little effort to disguise his work, and when reporters visited the site, they found it strewn with body parts. The public was outraged and shocked.

The city of Denver fired McGovern and ordered that any bodies still on the site after 90 days remain there. After 90 days, between 2000 and 3000 bodies had been unclaimed. The city covered the ground with grass and trees, eager to forget the scandal. Landscape architect Richard Schuetze was hired to design the park in 1898 and he began drawing up plans for a Greek pavilion and winding paths. Unfortunately, the city couldn't afford the pavilion, at least not until unpopular local millionaire Walter Cheesman died in 1907. His wife donated the $100,000 necessary to fund the pavilion's construction; in exchange, she asked that the city name the park after her husband.

It wasn't long before Cheesman Park became the center-piece of a suburban neighborhood of grand manors for the wealthy children of Denver's Capital Hill elite. But life in Cheesman Park wasn't nearly as comfortable as these scions might have hoped. Area residents began reporting that ghosts were haunting their homes, appearing out of thin air looking quite confused and lost. People looking in mirrors have seen, along with their own reflection, that of an individual they've never seen before. Whirling around to look behind them, they find they are alone, and the figure in the mirror is gone.

If the spirits aren't haunting these homes, then they haunt the park. A number of people have gone to Cheesman Park for a picnic and enjoyed themselves under the sun, only to find that they are unable to leave. Many have reported that an unseen force pushed down on them, preventing them from standing up. A man once fled the park, claiming a ghost had jumped on his back. When the moon is full, the park is transformed—the ground reflected in the moonlight illuminates the outlines of the original cemetery's graves.

Today, the spirits are still restless, a constant reminder of one man's disregard for the dead. Psychic sensitives walking through Cheesman Park feel saturated with confusion and sadness, while those who pass through late at night can hear a low moan coming from underneath the ground. It seems McGovern, in his disrespect for the bodies, had awakened the dead. His efforts to save money and move quickly—hacking off limbs and denying the dead a proper burial—roused the spirits from what should have been eternal slumber. They now roam the area, wondering why.

MICHIGAN
The Michigan Bell Building

This story is one selection from Dan Asfar's Ghost Stories of Michigan.

Many people who have worked, visited or studied in the Grand Rapids Michigan Bell building have long acknowledged that things are not quite right on the second floor. Some have reported the distinct feeling of being watched as they walked empty hallways—of a presence, malevolent and unseen, that causes the temperature in rooms to plummet, opens and closes doors, plays with light switches and moves ceiling tiles. One employee was walking to the elevator at the end of his day when he noticed a young woman he had never seen before standing on the stairs. He stopped and was just about to ask her who she was when she vanished into thin air.

Rumor has it that workers in the Michigan Bell building have grown so uncomfortable on the second story, that the telephone company has vacated the entire floor. While no one ever hits the "2" button on the elevator anymore, there has been more than one instance when the lift stops there anyway. The doorway opens, and for several tense moments the person on the elevator stares into the darkened hallway before the door closes again. Some witnesses claim to have caught a glimpse of a terror-stricken woman running from an unseen assailant just before the door slides shut. Some have frantically opened the door to assist the woman, only to find the hallway deserted and deadly quiet.

The origin of the tortured spirits that haunt the halls of Michigan Bell's second floor is believed to be buried in the history of Grand Rapids. It is a gruesome story of domestic violence that goes back to 1907, when an ill-fated young

The Michigan Bell building is host to many mysterious and eerie events, all seemingly focused on the second floor.

couple moved into town from Detroit, hoping to make a new start in the bustling young city.

Warren and Virginia Randall rented a house downtown on the corner of Davidson and Fountain Streets shortly after arriving in Grand Rapids. While we cannot know what kind of relationship the couple had in Detroit, or even during the first year in their new home, things went tragically wrong after Warren was crippled in a gruesome workplace accident in 1908. Working as a brakeman for the Grand Rapids and Indiana Railroad, the young man was standing in the wrong place when a car derailed; he ended up losing his leg in the ensuing carnage. Things got hellish in the Randall household after that.

Warren could not come to terms with his new wooden leg. Everywhere he looked, all he saw were the limitations of his sudden handicap, and it was not long before the workings of his mind changed to match the misshapen lurch of his one-legged gait. Virginia Randall received the brunt of his vicious insecurities.

We have no way of knowing if Virginia grew distant after Warren's accident, but it is quite apparent that he became convinced his young wife was unfaithful. Neighbors reported frightful rows coming from the Randall household as he started giving voice to his jealous neuroses evermore frequently. His roaring accusations were heard down the entire block and soon everyone was whispering about Virginia's trysts with the fruit vendor, with the local butcher—with every man Warren could think of. Things got so bad that on one night, Warren was spotted chasing his wife down the street with a straight razor, threatening to kill her. Virginia finally left Warren early in the month of August 1910.

Who knows what Warren promised Virginia, but he lured her out on the evening of August 26. It was a fine night, and after the couple went on a carriage ride, they ended up back at their old home. What transpired next will forever remain a mystery, but at some point after they had closed the door of their rooming house behind them, Warren must have decided that life was not worth living.

Postmortem investigations revealed that Warren had clubbed Virginia to death with his wooden leg. He then dragged her into the bedroom, locked the door, stuffed towels in every opening in the room and then unscrewed a gas fixture in the wall, flooding the room with deadly fumes. It seems that this death by asphyxiation was not working fast enough for Warren. He slit his own throat with a straight razor before the gas killed him.

Nobody gave any thought to the heavy silence that had descended on the Randall house until about two weeks later, when the neighbors noticed a ghastly stench coming from the place. Members from the Board of Health and the gas company were sent to investigate. Upon opening the front door to the house, all the agents present recoiled in disgust at the combined stench of gas and decay. By the time the police were called in and broke into the couple's old bedroom, both the corpses were blackened by rot. Warren could be identified only by his wooden leg.

No one moved into the house after the discovery in the bedroom. The entire neighborhood was aware of an oppressive foreboding that hung in the air around the place. Stories of strange noises coming from within began to circulate only days after the corpses were taken out of the house. Strange cries were heard in the middle of the night, and lights were seen flickering on and off. Parents had taken to telling their kids not to play anywhere near the Randall house. It was one of those rare bits of parental advice that children actually take to heart; indeed, the air of evil that hung over the place was so thick that even adventurous kids steered clear of it.

Under consistent pressure from nearby residents, the city finally demolished the house in 1920 and for a while at least, the Randall ghosts were quiet. That changed in 1924 when the Michigan Bell Telephone Company bought the empty lot and put up their own building. There have been reports of strange occurrences on the second floor ever since the Michigan Bell building was erected. People have attributed the thumping sounds, moving objects and cold presence to the incident at the Randall house almost from the outset. The young woman seen by some employees, usually at the end of their working day, is assumed to be Virginia Randall. And the phone calls being made from the second floor to Grand Rapids residents in the middle of the night, phone calls of frantic unintelligible whispering abruptly cut off by a disconnecting line—could those, as well, be calls from Virginia, forever reliving the last terrifying moments of her life? Many believe so.

LOUISIANA
St. Louis Cathedral

The year was 1762. The French, engaged in conflict with the British for control of the North American continent, were faring poorly in the waning days of the French-Indian Wars. Hopes for success were diminishing with each passing day, and France began taking measures to curb British influence. Desperate not to have their possessions in the south fall entirely into British hands, France signed the Treaty of Fontainebleau in 1762, ceding to Spain all territory west of the Mississippi as well as what was called the Isle of Orleans. When the Treaty of Paris was signed in 1763, Great Britain was only given control of all Louisiana east of the Mississippi, save for the Isle of Orleans. France's gambit did check British power, as New Orleans grew into a major port and trading center and its geography allowed it to control access to that great artery of commerce, the Mississippi River. But the cession of territory ignored those settlers in and around New Orleans who had emigrated under the fleur-de-lis. Their concerns were secondary, and their displeasure would find voice in revolution. They also found comfort in a trusted priest, who continues to minister to the faithful, even in death.

New Orleans was founded in 1718 by Jean Baptiste le Moyne, Sieur de Bienville, the governor of the French colony of Louisiana. Adrien de Pauger, an engineer, arrived in the city in 1721. He began laying out plans for the French Quarter,

The spirit of a beloved priest from the 18th century haunts New Orleans'
St. Louis Cathedral.

making sure to lay aside space for the construction of a church. The church would be dedicated to Louis IX, sainted King of France. A succession of French governors from Perier to Bienville to Vaudreuil attended mass there, alongside the children of both colonists and slaves. Over a hundred of them are buried under the floor. The prevailing belief at the time was that being buried under the church would bring the dead closer to heaven. The belief now is that the ghost of a bishop still watches over his former parishioners. He is always silent as he observes from the altar. On rainy days, though, he will sing, filling the air with a mournful kyrie, an elegy for the victims of a resistance.

Spain gained control of New Orleans in 1762, but did not send an official to govern the city until 1766. When French colonists realized what had happened, they protested, rebelling against the new Spanish regime. After two years of protest, ineffectual Spanish governor Don Antonio Uloa was ousted from power. Realizing the threat of the insurrection, Spain dispatched a new governor in 1769, an Irish mercenary named Don Alejandro O'Reilly, more colorfully remembered today as Bloody O'Reilly.

O'Reilly came to New Orleans determined to quell the insurrection. He had at his disposal 24 ships and a force of 3000 men, which outnumbered the entire free adult male population of New Orleans. In short order, O'Reilly had routed out the French leaders with little opposition. To set an example and establish a deterrent, he ordered the deaths of six French aristocrats. Five were shot by a firing squad, and the last was stabbed to death with a bayonet. O'Reilly decreed that the bodies would lie exposed to the elements and rot. For the French Catholics of New Orleans, the act was not only a gross violation of tradition but also the greatest of insults. But O'Reilly was determined to serve notice that he would not tolerate disorder.

St. Louis Church would not allow the bodies to rot. The executed men had attended the church for years and had been close with the pastor, Père Dagobert. Dagobert had embraced all worshippers—Spanish, Creole, French or American—in accordance with his belief that all were equal in the eyes of God and that everyone, regardless of their pasts, deserved a proper burial. O'Reilly's order was an affront against everything Dagobert stood for. The governor may have executed six men, but he could not suffocate the human spirit as easily.

In defiance, Dagobert and two other priests took it upon themselves to perform a proper religious service for the dead at the St. Louis Church and then laid the bodies to rest in St. Louis Cemetery No. 1. Dagobert led a procession in rain from the church to St. Peter Street, singing a kyrie along the way to comfort and support the mourners. Dagobert was lauded and praised, a hero to his parish.

The colonists never forgot Père Dagobert, even as New Orleans prospered under Spanish rule. Neither did the Spanish, it seems. When the second of two great fires swept through New Orleans in 1794, the St. Louis Church was destroyed. It was a Spaniard, Don Andres Almonester de Roxas, who spent a small fortune reconstructing the city including the St. Louis Church.

Today, the St. Louis Church is the St. Louis Cathedral, the oldest cathedral in the United States. Its three spires soar above Jackson Square. Both French and Spanish are interred within the church, finding in death a reconciliation with a bloody past. But lest the lessons of history be forgotten, Père Dagobert continues to walk the grounds even now. It's said that on days when rain falls from the heavens, Dagobert's mournful song can still be heard in the square, a lament for the fallen.

NEBRASKA
The State Capitol Building

No one is really sure exactly when it began, but over the last few decades, the sound of a lone man sobbing atop the State Capitol Building in Lincoln, Nebraska, has become something of an attraction. People have been coming up to the observation deck on the dome of Nebraska's state capitol for years. School field trips, tourists, couples on dates and people just looking to kill a day—countless observers have taken in the view of Lincoln sprawling below the legislature building's dome. But locals' attention started being diverted from the vista of the corn husker capital city when they began hearing a faint weeping. It was a strange sound, clear if one listened carefully enough, but somehow distant, as if heard from the end of a long tunnel. Yet the soulful wails seemed to be coming from all around—very near, yet unfathomably distant. The first people to hear the cries thought that someone on the observation deck was in trouble, but thorough searches of the walkway on the dome never yielded a thing.

Word spread that there was an invisible weeper on the top of the Capitol Building, and more visitors started to appear on the dome, straining their ears for a trace of a sound. To be sure, there were many who didn't hear the sounds but enough could discern the piteous cries coming from the very air, and the tale of the sobs on the Capitol Building began to gain currency.

It was not long before the human need to explain the inexplicable sent the curious to the newspaper archives and history books, where it was discovered that there is more to Nebraska's Capitol Building than policy debate and legislation. Indeed, enough tragedy has transpired there to make a grown man cry, or enough to send a wayward spirit into tears, anyway.

In the frigid December of 1968, a single man was strapped into a rope harness, hanging from a cord tied to the Capitol's dome. He was engaged in what was probably the least enviable yuletide duty in all of Lincoln: stringing up Christmas lights on the rounded roof of the Capitol Building. Dangling from a rope on a dome 13 stories above ground in a brisk winter wind, the man was not happy about his current place in the world; in fact, he was petrified.

It was horrible work, and no one in Lincoln was too eager to volunteer for the service. So it became a tradition to offer the job to inmates at the state penitentiary. Those who signed up for the task were usually looked on favorably on their next parole board review. That was until 1968, when the last convict was to perform the yearly ritual.

No one knows for certain if the convict had a weak heart or if he suffered from an inordinate fear of heights, but the prison guard who was watching over the man as he crawled across the dome was struck by how slowly he was moving. His steps, short and tentative, were so pathetic the guard stuck his head out onto the roof to see what the problem was. It was then, in the dim moonlight, that he saw the look on the man's face. There was no question the prisoner was struggling with a debilitating terror. His face was contorted into tearful horror as he tried, unsuccessfully, to contain mortified sobs. The guard did not have a chance to say a word to his stricken ward. In the next instant, the man's entire body convulsed violently and he looked suddenly surprised, as if hit with a sudden realization; a moment later, he was dead. The coroner's report revealed that the convict had suffered a massive heart attack as he hung from that rope, unable to deal with what must have been a virulent fear of heights.

Many have linked this convict's fear-filled demise with the mysterious sobbing on the observation deck. It is believed that the terror this man felt during his last moments was so intense, it somehow engraved itself into a psychic space on the dome. As a result, these sobs, the plaintive expression of the convict's mortal dread, are forever being replayed, faintly heard in the material realm by visitors to the Capitol Building today.

The other prevalent theory regarding the sobbing on the dome involves an event that took place in the late 1950s, when a heartbroken Nebraskan wandered up the legislative building right after breaking up with his girlfriend. Today, the long spiral staircase he walked up to get to the roof is closed to the public, barred by a wired gate that is usually locked. The staircase has been restricted for many years; it does not have a central support beam, so a person leaning too far over the inside rail could fall, unobstructed, for 13 stories. This is precisely what happened to the poor man who stumbled up the staircase in a desperate attempt to rise above his troubles. Some say he jumped once he reached the top, others believe he tumbled over the rail accidentally. Whatever the case, he fell from the very top, plummeting the 13 stories and dying instantly when he hit the ground. The staircase was sealed off soon after. Could the weeping be this man's sorrowful moans just before he fell to his death?

With these two tragedies to pick from, no one is sure exactly who is sobbing at the top of the Capitol Building. But there is even more unsettling information regarding Lincoln's legislative building. It is rumored that long before Nebraska was settled, local American Indians considered the hill the building is constructed upon hallowed ground. Many people claim to have felt a horrible chill in the lowest floors of the Capitol Building and are haunted by a distinct sense that they shouldn't be there. Those who have experienced this feeling in the basement have never again been comfortable anywhere in the legislature. It was as if they were told by some inaudible voice that they were not welcome there— that they would never be welcome. Perhaps, then, the entire Capitol Building is haunted, charged with the negative energy of disconsolate Indian spirits, upset by the fact that their holy ground has not been treated with the proper respect. Maybe it is this negative energy that gives voice to the miserable spirits who lost their lives on the top floor, who continue to sob out of mortal fear or inconsolable heartbreak, sending futile wails into an indifferent Nebraska sky.

TEXAS
The Alamo

The Alamo is one of America's premier historical landmarks. Built by Franciscan monks in 1718, the monastery was converted into an altar of American democracy on March 6, 1836, when General Antonio Lopez de Santa Anna gave the order that sent 4000 Mexican soldiers charging towards the nearly 200 Texan men garrisoned inside. Almost everyone knows the outcome of the frantic hour-and-a-half battle, where all but a handful of Texans were killed in the most publicized last stand in military history. Since that dramatic battle of the Texas Revolution, "Remember the Alamo!" has become a rallying cry for beleaguered American troops wherever they might be, bolstering soldiers' courage in the heat of battle. And so the spirit of the Alamo continues to live on, occupying an important place in the mythos of a dauntless American democracy, resolved to remain vigilant in the face of any enemy before it.

Yet as many San Antonio residents know, the spirit of the Alamo lives on in more ways than one: the fort is deemed one of the most haunted sites in the state of Texas. Perhaps it is the historical significance of the Texans' sacrifice in the old Franciscan monastery. The men who fell in the fort, their deaths imbued with a timeless significance for the entire nation, have taken on an aspect of timelessness themselves, continuing to haunt the hallowed ground where they gave their lives for an independent Texas and an American ideal. Or it may be the sheer horror of so many individuals' final moments, where the defenders saw imminent death arriving on dark wings by crashing cannon, whistling musket ball and glinting bayonet—no quarter asked, none given. It could be that the merciless fighting that March 6 morning almost 200 years ago was so vicious that some of the combatants remain behind, unable to come to terms with the brutality of their final end.

Either way, things have never been the same at the Alamo since 1836. Strange happenings began occurring there soon after the legendary battle. It was April 21, 1836, when Santa Anna surrendered to the Texans after a decisive defeat at the Battle of San Jacinto. Before he submitted, Santa Anna gave the Mexican garrison in San Antonio orders to destroy the Alamo's chapel, a final strike against his Texan enemies before he retreated south past the Rio Grande. But the soldiers sent out to destroy the occupied building were never able to carry out the command.

According to legend, the contingent of Mexicans ordered to raze the Alamo were stopped at the entrance by a terrifying sight. Six ghostly, semitransparent soldiers stood in a half circle before the chapel door, each holding a flaming saber aloft. It was evening, and a hot orange light from the phantoms' upraised weapons flickered over the bizarre scene. The only way into the building for the Mexicans was through the six

One of the most haunted sites in Texas

figures that were standing in their way, but not a man among them was able to take a single step towards the fort, so terrified were they of the defiant apparitions. There is no historical record of who these spirits were. It was too dark, and they were encased in too much shadow for anyone to make out any features. The soldiers stood before the phantoms for a few minutes before the resolve of one of the Mexicans finally broke. Telling his shaking comrades they could fight *los diablos* if they wished, he turned his back to the Alamo and headed back to his barracks. The rest of the men weren't far behind him.

This was only the first story to come out of the fort. Soon after, people started taking notice of a solitary figure that appeared atop the Alamo on some nights, moving from east to west on the south side of the roof. Some described the figure as a lone sentry, deliberately making his rounds over an anachronistic post. Others swear that there is a desperate cadence to the figure's movements, as if it is frantically look-ing for some sort of escape. Whatever the case, those who have actually gone on to the roof to investigate have never gotten a chance to inquire what the mysterious individual might be up to, for no one has ever seen him face to face.

San Antonio was using the Alamo as police headquarters through the 1890s, during which time countless officers heard the footsteps making their way across the roof of the building. Time and again, officers climbed up to see who was walking around on the roof, but there was never anyone there. After countless visitations by this mysterious rooftop interloper, policemen blamed it on the weather, explaining the footsteps away by surmising that the sounds could be caused by rain or falling objects blown in by the wind. While no one really believed these rationalizations, they helped a little bit in easing the officers' minds. The apparition of the solitary figure atop the Alamo continues to be spotted today by San Antonio tourists and residents alike, a lone man con-tinuing his timeless walk across the roof, motivated by a force that may forever remain a mystery.

This nocturnal figure isn't the only remnant of the 19th century that continues to haunt the Alamo. Another legend concerns a small fortune said to be buried in the wall of the southwest corner of the fort. According to this account, the Alamo's defenders placed all their personal treasures in one of the Alamo's bells just before the siege began and buried it under the fort. Many mediums who have claimed to com-municate with the spirits of the dead Texans in the fort have confirmed this story. And according to some, it is no paltry treasure. One psychic has stated that over $540,000 in gold is hidden beneath the fort.

Yet unless the state of Texas is willing to take a wrecking ball to the historical site, the existence of this treasure must remain in question, a legend rather than a fact, along with all the other supernatural tales regarding the celebrated building.

Visitors today continue to experience disturbing events at the Alamo. There are many accounts of sudden cold spots in the long barracks building, the reputed site of the fiercest fighting. Lone tourists have also heard harsh whispers hissing at them from empty space. And then there are those who have heard the brisk tramp of numerous marching feet, of painful moans carried on the ether, coming from everywhere and nowhere.

Such experiences, and all stories associated with them, are usually pigeonholed as folklore or supernatural phenomena, largely disassociated from the formal history of the fort. Nevertheless, they have proven the test of time, and over 150 years after the first supernatural experience was reported in the fort, ghost stories still abound, making the historic Alamo one of the most haunted buildings in San Antonio, if not the entire state of Texas.

3
Haunted
Countryside

CONNECTICUT
Dudleytown

Dudleytown lies in the hills of northwest Connecticut, veiled in the permanent shadow of thick forest and looming landscape, located deep within an eternal dusk that scares even woodland creatures. There is little left of the small settlement now; its wooded surroundings, dark and still, have turned what was a town into abandoned ruins, which only the brave of heart and obstinately curious bother to visit.

Established by a man named Thomas Griffis in 1739, Dudleytown was one of those American villages that never really became what its founders might have hoped. Another ghost town among the countless abandoned communities pockmarked across the United States, Dudleytown has long since fallen prey to the encroaching wilderness. The old buildings that used to house stubborn 18th-century frontiersmen have been reduced to crumbling foundations overgrown with moss and weed. The cellar holes of these homes are now damp caverns in the ground where centipedes and rodents live among the winding tree roots that break out of the underground walls, floor and ceiling.

But Dudleytown is hardly just another ghost town slowly succumbing to the forces of nature. One visit to the long-deserted community is all it takes to realize that something is very wrong in that verdurous stretch of wilderness. There is a distinct, intangible sense that people don't belong, that the woods would rather be left undisturbed to brood over some mysterious secret. Some have felt it as a heavy weight on the chest, as if an enormous hand is tightening its grip around individuals' lungs, squeezing the breath out of hapless visitors. Others talk about the leaden stillness in and around Dudleytown, where not a hare, squirrel or vole makes a sound; the stillness is such that there are those who believe that wildlife avoid the place all together, instinctively shunning the ominous wood out of some deeper wisdom humans cannot grasp.

Given the eventual fate of many of those who attempted to settle in the area, pioneers would have done better if they were imbued with this same wisdom. For the horrific history of Dudleytown only confirms the dreadful feel in the air around the village ruins. Murder, insanity, strange sightings on the edge of town, vanishing townsfolk, suicides, epidemics and freakish deaths—those who moved to the cursed settlement in the wood were visited with a morbid plethora of lethal difficulties. Only after Dudleytowners packed up and left, virtually driven out by these rampant hostile forces, did the tragedies abate, replaced by the eerie silence that reigns over the area today.

The long string of tragedies that made up the chronicle of Dudleytown began in August 1774, about 35 years after the town was founded. An unknown illness swept through the home of a settler by the name of Adoniram Carter, infecting his entire family. The entire house was bedridden for about a week, until the strange disease claimed them all in the same day. It is still not clear what they died from. The dismal march of death and insanity in Dudleytown had begun.

Adoniram's brother, Nathaniel, was as grief-ridden as he was frightened by the sudden demise of his brother's household, and he moved his wife and children from Dudleytown to New York. They had not been in their new home long when Indians raided their farm, killing Nathaniel, his wife and one of his children. The Indian marauders took the other three children as prisoners.

A few years later, Revolutionary General Heman Swift would be the next town resident to deal with the mortal tragedy. Swift's wife was standing on their front porch during a stormy day when she was struck by lightning, killed in a flashing instant on her very doorstep. While anyone would expect General Swift to be affected by such a sudden and meaningless death of a loved one, his transformation after the loss of his wife made many uneasy. Not long after Mrs. Swift was buried, the general began to rant about strange shapes in the woods, horrible hoofed monsters that moved swiftly, only stopping long enough to leer at him through the dense foliage. It was at this time that settlers' livestock began to mysteriously disappear without a trace. General Swift was seen on many nights standing by himself on the edge of town, stiff as a statue, staring intently into the dark forest. There were nights when he would not move until the sun began to rise. Everyone believed that he had gone mad.

Dementia was a common problem in Dudleytown. Over the course of its history, there were numerous accounts of villagers suddenly slipping into states of paranoid delusion, chronic distraction or indolent torpor. The sounds and shadows of the surrounding woods claimed the minds of many. An all-too-frequent indicator that another resident had fallen into insanity was an obsessive interest in what was transpiring in the surrounding trees. During particularly dark times, one could find a handful of townsfolk standing at the forest's edge, staring blankly at some unknown sight within.

Tales of these strange goings-on in the small town of Dudleytown began to spread. People in nearby Cornwall whispered about a curse hanging over the isolated town. There was talk of the town being built over a Mohawk burial ground. Many believed that the spirits of disconsolate Indians were responsible for the evil that was transpiring in town.

Others believed that living breathing Mohawks were largely responsible for the unfortunate events that were occurring.

Years passed, and life remained as difficult as ever in the small town in the hills. No farms could be planted on the rocky ground, livestock disappeared regularly and people, as well, had a disturbing tendency to simply vanish. In 1892, madness claimed another town resident, John Brophy, after his young wife died suddenly and his two children disappeared into the woods, never to be found again.

The stories started to discourage people from settling in Dudleytown. Throughout the 19th century, more and more townsfolk moved out of the troubled village, until only a handful of stubborn settlers were left at the turn of the century. By the 1930s, the town was all but deserted, its old houses crumbling vestiges of a miserable past, the implacable woods reclaiming the ground that was once theirs.

There is one more account of a man moving into Dudleytown, enraptured with the idea of solitude in the hills of Connecticut. He was a New York doctor named William Clarke, and in 1937 he decided to make a holiday home near the old ghost town. It was a grave mistake. According to local legend, he and his wife were vacationing near Dudleytown when the doctor was called in for an emergency. Clarke went back to New York for two days—48 hours—all the time it took for the town of Dudleytown to work its dark magic. When Dr. Clarke returned, he found his wife huddled in the upstairs bedroom, babbling incoherently about the creatures in the woods. Whatever events had transpired when Clarke was gone, they were enough to have driven his wife completely mad. He got her all the help he could, but to no avail. A few weeks after her two-day stay in Dudleytown, Mrs. Clarke had committed suicide. No one has lived in Dudleytown since.

Today, many theories are offered in an attempt to explain the history of the cursed town. The rationally minded emphasize concrete factors: Mohawk Indians are said to be responsible for the disappearance of people and livestock; a high lead content in the water or the consumption of tainted rye is believed to have caused the high incidence of insanity. Others, however, have different theories. Referred to as a "dead zone" by some researchers, Dudleytown is said to be situated in a negative energy zone, one of many on the planet, which are able to attract an inordinate number of negative spirits. There is also the legend of the Dudleytown curse, which tells of an ancient hex placed on the Dudley forefathers in the 16th century for their role in the attempted overthrow of King Henry VIII. It is believed that the town inherited this curse when the three Dudley brothers—who gave the town its name—Gideon, Barzillai and Abiel, moved into town in 1753.

The people who expound these supernatural theories point to the strange occurrences that continue today, mentioning the heavy feeling in the air, the unnatural silence of the woods and the bizarre figures occasionally spotted in forest. One famous account has a local television crew filming a black silhouette emerging from the stone foundations of one of the ruined houses. Other people walking through the area tell of the strange feeling that the ground was somehow grabbing onto them, disabling any movement. All this disagreement has turned the abandoned town into something of a controversy.

Have natural, explicable forces ruined Dudleytown? Or are there darker, supernatural explanations for what has transpired there? Either way, one can still sense the oppressive air of tragedy that hangs in the branches of the dark hills, can almost feel the loss, pain and heartache that consumed so many early Americans who settled in the doomed town so many years ago.

Wyoming
Fort Laramie

In the mid-1800s, tensions between settlers and the Plains Indians had reached their breaking point, as the Indians resented the settlers' increasing encroachment upon their ancestral lands. Congress wanted to protect the settlers and approved the construction of forts along the Oregon Trail, each manned by a regiment of mounted riflemen. Laramie, founded in 1849, was the second of these forts. Laramie became the gateway to the Northwest and was fondly referred to as the "Queen of the Frontier Forts." For years, Fort Laramie was all that stood between order and chaos along the plains. Even after the wave of settlers receded, troops were needed to inspect and defend the recently completed transcontinental telegraph line of 1861.

When swarms of prospectors and miners rushed to the gold fields of the Black Hills, violating a number of terms established in the Treaty of 1868, the Sioux, who kept the hills as sacred land, were incensed and waged a war to drive off the intruders. Fort Laramie became the staging point for the United States Army's counteroffensives. By the end of the 1880s, however, Fort Laramie had outlived its usefulness. Relative peace and harmony settled upon the plains. The fort was decommissioned in 1890 and its buildings auctioned off to civilians.

Today Fort Laramie is a National Historic Site, popular with tourists longing to catch a glimpse of a time when the West had not yet been won, when the frontier was a place where life was cheap and only the fittest—or those with the best aim—survived. There are all indications that more than just the fort's buildings have been preserved at Fort Laramie.

Fort Laramie is a National Historic Site visited by tourists—and ghosts.

Earl Murray, writing in *Ghosts of the Old West*, describes a variety of encounters that one former employee had during his years at the fort. Mike Caligione worked at Fort Laramie from 1971 to 1985. "After so many years out here," Caligione said, "you don't say anything, because people would think you were batty, but I've seen them and so have others."

Included among Mike's various duties was the closing and locking of the heavy doors to what used to be the captain's quarters, Quarter A. Each night, Caligione would perform this task, make his rounds and then return to Quarter A only to find the doors unlocked, standing wide open. There were times he thought someone might have been playing a trick on him, but then there were those nights in late fall and early winter when there were no visitors at the fort and Mike was the only living person there. Caligione also described how he would hear noises coming from the second floor, but when he investigated, he could find nothing responsible for the sounds.

The Woman in Green rides her ghostly horse across the plains near this fort.

The incidents scared Caligione, for he could find no explanation for their occurrences; he suspected that the fort was haunted. His suspicions were confirmed when he was grabbed and slapped by an invisible being. But, rather than run from the problem, Caligione confronted it. Refusing to deal with a nameless entity, Caligione christened his particular spirit George. He would address it, asking George not to interfere with his duties. The tactic worked. George's mischievous spirit was tamed…well, almost. There were still times where Caligione had to remind his guest about keeping the doors closed.

George is not the only spirit adding excitement and mystery to the atmosphere at Fort Laramie. The Woman in Green was seen as early as the middle of the 19th century, when soldiers stationed at Fort Laramie first witnessed the strange phenomenon. In 1871, Lieutenant James Nicholas Allison, the fort's new cavalry commander, set out from Fort Laramie with a group of fellow soldiers to hunt wolves. At some point, Allison was separated from the group, and he found himself alone in the windswept plains. Or was he? Riding across a long hill in the distance was a woman in a green dress atop a black stallion. Thinking the woman might be in trouble, Allison gave chase. But try as he might, he could gain no ground. She disappeared over a small rise and when Allison gained the mount, he looked out over the prairie and saw nothing. The woman had vanished.

A shaken Allison returned to the fort where he related to the other soldiers what had happened. To his surprise and relief, they nodded in recognition. They told him he had seen the Woman in Green, the spirit of an officer's daughter who appears every seven years upon the plains. Allison learned that in life, the woman had chosen a suitor her father did not approve of. Disobeying her father, she would ride from the fort for hours until one night, she never returned home. No one knew her fate, but it wasn't long before the Sioux and other tribal bands began to tell the story of the vanishing woman in green. Soldiers at Fort Laramie witnessed the same phenomenon and it became painfully clear that the daughter had met an untimely fate and would now spend an eternity riding the plains, going nowhere, appearing only every seven years to pique the curiosity and arouse interest.

Other spirits at Fort Laramie are not as shy as the Woman in Green. In 1985, two young girls were sitting and chatting on the upper balcony of Old Bedlam, the fort's post quarters. Their conversation was interrupted when a rapping at the window behind them caught their attention. There, in the window, was a man dressed in a cavalry officer's uniform. "Be quiet," he ordered, "we're trying to have a meeting." The moment the words left his mouth, the officer vanished. The two girls stared in shock at the window before retreating down the stairs.

Officer's Quarters A, in haunted Fort Laramie

Visitors to Fort Laramie feel the undeniable pull of history as they walk its grounds. After all, it's difficult to resist history's gravity when the sounds of heavy boots can be heard treading over the boardwalk in front of the cavalry barracks, like soldiers answering reveille, but no one is seen marching. The past truly comes to life in this grandest of frontier forts, sometimes with a vibrancy and vitality unsettling to the unprepared visitor.

MONTANA
Reno's Crossing

Custer's last stand is the stuff of legend, still capable of spawning great debate. Was he a victim of his own recklessness or a victim of circumstance? On June 26, 1876, Colonel George Armstrong Custer led his men into the Little Big Horn Valley, determined to bring all remaining Sioux and Cheyenne onto the Great Sioux Reservation. It was an act of avarice, motivated by the discovery of gold in the Black Hills. Unfortunately, the federal government was unable to reap the benefits; the Fort Laramie Treaty of 1868 guaranteed the Black Hills to the Indians. The government attempted to buy the land from the treaty chiefs but were denied their prize when those who refused to recognize the treaty, among them Crazy Horse and Black Moon, obstructed the negotiations. If the renegades could be brought to their knees, then the government could seize control of the Black Hills. Of course, the doing proved much more difficult than the planning. All five companies under Custer's command were destroyed; not a man survived. His other two battalions, under Captain Frederick W. Benteen and Major Marcus A. Reno, fared slightly better.

Reno was instructed to attack from the east while Custer came from the north. Reno did surprise the village camped along the Little Big Horn River, but the advantage soon faded as the Indians' superior numbers overwhelmed the army. Reno and his men took cover in the thick trees standing along the banks. They struggled to hold their line, but the futility of their efforts forced Reno to issue a retreat to the high bluffs lining the eastern side of the river. The movement was clumsy and disorganized and the Indians were quick to press their advantage. Many American soldiers were killed as they fled in panic down the Little Big Horn River; the waters ran red with the blood of the dead and dying. The site is now known simply as Reno's Crossing, an innocuous name that hints little at the terror and carnage visited here so many years ago.

One soldier, known as Benny to his friends, as Second Lieutenant Benjamin Hodgson to others, was brought down from his mount when a bullet shattered his leg and killed his horse. He was dragged from the river to shore and despite the blinding pain in his leg, managed to drag his weary and battered body up the banks before he was shot again and killed. His body rolled back down into the river from which he had just escaped. A marker here at the spot reminds people today of where Hodgson died.

The Little Bighorn National Monument marks the field of battle where Custer engaged the Indian forces. Five miles away is Reno's Crossing. The landscape is pristine and undisturbed, isolated swaths of rolling prairie lands covering 765 protected acres. A walk along Last Stand Hill and near Custer National Cemetery is often accompanied by an overwhelming sense of sorrow and loss. Little has changed here since Custer's last stand and even today, the echoes of the past continue to make themselves heard.

Earl Murray, writing in *Ghosts of the Old West*, describes the experiences an intern had while working at the Little Bighorn National Monument. In 1983 Christine Hope was a student intern from Minnesota who gave lectures on the history of the park. She lived in an apartment at the edge of Custer National Cemetery, the final resting place for over 5000 men.

One evening, she awoke suddenly, unable to ignore the sense of dread gnawing away at her. Looking around her room, she noticed a man sitting in her easy chair. Hope was terrified; she lived alone and felt herself at the mercy of the intruder. But a strange calm soon replaced her fears, and as she looked at the stranger, she lost herself in his gaze, in the eyes tinged with melancholy and fear. Although she couldn't say where, she felt as if she had seen this man before. In fact, his hair and handlebar mustache mirrored closely those she had seen when studying photographs of soldiers who had died at the Battle of Little Bighorn. The figure then did a most puzzling and surprising thing—he vanished, disappearing into the air like breath on a cold winter's day. When she awoke the next morning, Hope could not be sure of what had happened. Had it all been just a dream?

That afternoon, she and a fellow park ranger walked along Reno's Crossing. At the edge of the Little Big Horn River, at the bottom of a steep embankment, was a marker, one of many placed throughout the site to honor the fallen soldier. Hope noted the name on this particular monument: Second Lieutenant Benjamin H. Hodgson. Back at the visitors' center, she sought to find Hodgson's photo. She came across a book, long out of print, that detailed the military biographies of those who had fallen at Reno's Crossing. When she found Hodgson's, she trembled when she saw the reproduction of his faded daguerreotype. There, staring from the pages of this yellowing book, were the eyes of the man she'd glimpsed in her moonlit bedroom. He had found her the night before, and now she had found him. Hope couldn't help feeling that in those eyes was a sorrow and resignation that begged to be embraced and not shunned. It was as if he were pleading for the lives of all those who had fought that day, both aboriginals and Americans.

It doesn't appear as if Hodgson is alone in that sentiment. Park ranger Mardell Plainfeather, a Crow Indian, was coming out of a sweat lodge next to the Little Big Horn River. The sky was clear, the stars were bright and the moon was full. And there, above her on a bluff, were the silhouetted figures of two Indian warriors on horseback. One dismounted and began to approach her. Not knowing why, Plainfeather retreated quickly. When she returned the next morning, she went up to the bluffs, looking for signs among the tall prairie grass for any trail that the two riders might have left. She found nothing, nothing to show that two riders had been on the bluff the night before. The bluff was clear of trees, presenting a flat horizon where little could be misconstrued to be a figure on horseback. Plainfeather didn't doubt what she saw; she was convinced she had seen the spirits of the departed. Deep within, she could sense their presence, beings who only meant to keep her company and safe from harm. Plainfeather offered a prayer to the dead as well as sage and sweet tobacco, to ease the pain of all who suffered so gravely on June 26, 1876.

Even in the silence, it seems the dead have voices still; theirs is a chorus far greater and bolder than the cacophony of gunfire, with a message of reconciliation that reaches more deeply than any bullet. In the Little Bighorn National Monument, the grievances of the past have been forgiven as former enemies embrace the humanity common within the hearts of all.

Utah
Dove Creek Camp

On May 10, 1869, officials from both the Central Pacific and Union Pacific Railways met at Promontory Point, Utah. They were joined by a host of others, including bankers, dignitaries and railroad men, all of whom had gathered in the makeshift townsite for the conclusion of one of the grandest undertakings in American history: the completion of the transcontinental railroad. When the last spike was driven into the ties, the assembled crowd raised their voices in jubilation; major cities across the country were quick to join the revelries as telegraph spread word of the railroad's completion. A photograph was taken to commemorate the moment.

Unfortunately, the photo was at odds with the railroad's true history. Although the image faithfully recreates the moment when the final spike was driven home, a closer look shows none of the 13,000 Chinese railroad workers who, according to Stan Steiner, built road beds and laid tracks for half of the transcontinental line (as well as parts of practically every railroad line in the West). So unforgivable was the oversight that the ghosts of some of the workers still haunt the line near Promontory Point today.

The Pacific Railroad Act of 1862 set off a frenzy of construction, a mania fuelled by greed and competition. Two companies, the Central Pacific, beginning in Sacramento, California, and the Union Pacific from Omaha, Nebraska, began laying track with hopes of meeting somewhere in the West to connect the two. The act promised subsidy bonds and land grants to help the companies secure the funds necessary to lay track; basically, the more track a company laid, the more money it received from the government. Naturally,

Chinese rail workers who lived at Dove Creek Camp haunt the rail line.

both companies were eager to capitalize on the offer, and the owners of the companies recognized that hardworking, industrious and reliable laborers were necessary to win the race. But such men were in short supply.

Immigrants from China first started arriving in the West in the heady days of the gold rush, eager, like so many others, to amass stores of unimaginable wealth. Even as the gold rush began to fade, the Chinese still came by the tens of thousands, drawn by the possibilities for adventure in an exotic environment. But life was not simple. Work wasn't easy to find; they were given only the most loathsome tasks and seen as unfit for honest labor.

To their credit, the Chinese railway workers proved themselves tireless and efficient laborers. Soon enough, more were sent to blast and lay ties over the Sierras. Many died trying to conquer the heights, either falling from baskets suspended at the tops of cliffs or perishing in dynamite blasts. But they succeeded. By 1868, the Sierras had been surmounted and the vast plains of the interior lay open.

Yet when the railroad was completed, these workers and those who had died to bring the railroad to the West were forgotten. Shallow graves were all that the Chinese had to memorialize the dead. The number of dead is not known, but according to newspaper accounts of 1870, 20,000 pounds of bones had been gathered from the graves lining the roadbeds. It's not surprising, then, that some workers' spirits continue to linger alongside the fruits of their labors.

The once-thriving camp at Dove Creek near Promontory Point went bust as soon as the railroad was completed. Its population of Chinese laborers left to seek work elsewhere. Over the years, numerous reports of strange activity in the area have been collected by researchers such as Earl Murray. Steve Ellison, a historian and park ranger, described to Murray how one night, while patrolling the old Central Pacific Railroad grade, he suddenly heard behind him a chorus of voices and footsteps. He smothered his fear and forced himself to listen carefully. "There were voices, distinct voices. I came to the conclusion they were Chinese."

He clearly heard voices saying "A-melican," a word he associated with his Chinese landlady in San Francisco. She had referred to all Caucasians with the term, and Ellison now found himself the subject of the ghostly patter. Then, standing there in the darkness, he saw what he could only describe as sparks flying from the spikes and rails, "as if a hundred men were pounding at once." Even in death, the Chinese laborers continued to work, as if to remind the forgetful that their contributions should not be understated. Today, the ghosts of Dove Creek stand as testament to the sacrifice and dedication of thousands of workers who gave their lives and skills to their adopted homeland.

OREGON
The Bandage Man

Cannon Beach is a tiny municipality spread over a magnificent stretch of coastline in northern Oregon, located just off scenic Highway 101. The town's 1588 residents live along a four-mile beach that marks the boundaries of the burg. Most of Cannon Beach's townsfolk will readily agree that there are far worse places in the world to call home. The roaring waters of the Pacific Ocean are broken up by cloisters of craggy rocks jutting up off the shoreline before washing onto the soft sands of the northern beach. The unobstructed western horizon marks the flawless union of the oscillating ocean with the enormous sky. It is a beautiful corner of the country, a secluded getaway where many city dwellers go to escape the frantic pace of urban America.

But there is more to Cannon Beach than bucolic coastal charm. For years, a dark presence has hung over the community, haunting the quiet beach settlement after the sun goes down, a shuffling bloodstained humanoid horror that has been spotted along the shoulder of the 101 turnoff, lunging at anything or anybody brave, foolish or unfortunate enough to get in its way.

He is the Bandage Man, a reeking oddity that bears tragic resemblance to the classic Hollywood mummy. Swaddled in soiled cloth bandages that hang in tatters from stiff limbs, he has wandered the short stretch of road from the highway into town for as long as anyone can remember. He comes most often on those nights when lightning dances over the Pacific's white-capped waters and torrential rain pounds upon the windswept beach. It is then that visitors and townsfolk who are coming or going from Cannon Beach have spotted the limping figure in their headlights. The legend of the Bandage Man has become so widely circulated that few people who spot the misshapen form stop their vehicles. But those not warned of the malevolent tendencies of this bizarre being, who have pulled up to aid what they believe to be a distressed pedestrian, have invariably come under swift and brutal attack.

No one is certain about the origins of the Bandage Man, but whoever or whatever he is, the creature has an unmitigated hatred for all living beings. Some say that the roadside manifestation is the traumatized spirit of a logger who suffered a gruesome death in a local sawmill many years ago. It is said that he did not die immediately after he was diced up by the buzzing blade. Gravely wounded, he was wrapped in bandages from head to foot in an attempt to stop the bleeding, but still died of blood loss within the day. Another story has the Bandage Man being crushed under a landslide on the coast late in the 19th century. Whatever the case, the bloody creature is not happy about whatever horrible disaster claimed him and seems intent on taking out his anger on anyone around Cannon Beach.

The Bandage Man has been blamed for more than one atrocity along the haunted road into town. Legend has cast him as the guilty party in a number of murders that were reputed to have taken place in Cannon Beach's history. While none of these killings can be confirmed in official records and no victims have been found along the road in the recent past, the legend of the Bandage Man persists.

Macabre discoveries in the daylight hours have done much to keep the Bandage Man alive in the local folklore. People driving into town have often been distracted by the sight of something dead lying along the road. All sorts of animals have been discovered—dogs, deer, birds, cats—horribly mutilated, sometimes half-eaten, lying in a fleshy mess of gore on the concrete. While roadkill is a common sight along any highway in North America, tattered cloth bandages are often found around the dead animals outside Cannon Beach.

And then there are the sightings of the shambling horror himself. To this day, motorists have caught sight of a large bandaged man loping along the turnoff on rainy nights, making his way down the road with a grotesque gait. Some have claimed that the figure took notice of them, promptly veering to intercept the vehicle they were driving. Many of these unfortunate few have had the opportunity to see the Bandage Man in greater detail, describing hateful eyes gleaming under filthy bloodstained bandages, dirty fingernails protruding from bony, half-decomposed fingers and the sickening odor of rotting flesh.

Those who have gotten this close to the mummified monster have not been reticent about their terrifying experiences. And most of those hitchhiking or driving along Highway 101 on stormy nights have been especially careful when nearing the Cannon Beach turnoff. For many of these travelers, their vigilance has been rewarded by the sight of a loping man making his way through the stormy night, lumbering along the road on an eternal quest for vengeance against the living.

SOUTH CAROLINA
Baynard Plantation

In the storm it comes, hooves pounding down the path, the whole of it lit like a strobe by frenzied flashes of lightning, its arrival heralded by the deafening peals of thunder. It comes tearing through the black, a black coach drawn by four black horses, the black satin ribbons whipping and snapping behind it markers of death. Inside sits the apparition of a man long departed from this earth, a man with the broken heart and soul of the tortured lover, a man staring blankly from his carriage, eyes stained with the melancholy of loss. The carriage races along the South Carolina coast, running from a past that will not be forgotten, from a memory that will never fade. The past has been preserved here, here in the Low Country on Hilton Head Island.

Near the southern end of the island stand the Stoney-Baynard ruins, the last vestiges of what once was a great plantation, a grand example of the economy that continued to sustain the agricultural south as their neighbors to the north embraced industrialization. It was an economy built upon the backs of the oppressed, with slave owners rising to prominence and prosperity through the enslavement of others.

European settlers first began arriving here in 1525, although there is archaeological evidence to suggest that the area had been inhabited since 10,000 BC. Spanish sailors arrived on the coast of what would become South Carolina, naming the headland upon which they landed *La Ponta de Santa Elena*, known now as St. Helena, one of the oldest and continually used European names on the North American continent. The French vied early with the Spanish for occupation and in 1663, the English entered the fray.

English Captain William Hilton arrived on the island by way of Barbados on a search for tropical lands on which English plantations could be established. He found what he was looking for on this lush and beautiful island. Christening the place Hilton's Headland, he began encouraging settlement here immediately after the Spaniards and American Indians had been displaced. In 1670, a permanent settlement was established where the Ashley and Cooper rivers meet. Its settlers named it Charlestowne, now Charleston. They found that its rich soil allowed certain labor-intensive crops, such as cotton, rice, indigo and tobacco, to thrive. The climate had created new opportunities for wealth and a host of individuals came here to test their fortunes.

One such individual was Captain Jack Stoney, a patriot raider from the Revolutionary War. Using profits culled from years of looting British cargoes, he built a mansion, shunning brick and wood in favor of tabby, a mixture of oyster shells, sand and water. The mansion was the centerpiece of what was the largest plantation in Greensboro, comprising over 600 acres of fields dedicated to growing tobacco and cereals. Over 200 slaves might have been working the lands at any given time. Stoney lived here in opulence with his wife and family for 50 years. It's at this point where history merges with legend and the fascinating story of Baynard Plantation can truly be said to begin.

In 1843, William Eddings Baynard entered the Stoneys' life. Some believe he acquired the plantation on the strength of his poker-playing abilities, winning ownership in a hand of the game that proved unlucky for Captain Jack Stoney. Others, including writers Nancy Roberts and Terrance Zepke, offer a different explanation. Rather than losing his life's work, it's believed that Stoney gave the plantation to Baynard, a gift to the man who had captured the heart of his other life work, his beautiful daughter Victoria, a stunning vision with long black hair, deep green eyes and alabaster skin. In Baynard, Stoney had found a man who could run the plantation long after he had gone. But anticipation of the pending nuptials between Baynard and Victoria would only prove to be the prelude to tragedy.

It's unclear when exactly Victoria fell ill. But at a time when she should have been celebrating the beauty and ecstasy of true love, she was fighting for her life instead. The illness came quickly but not without warning, at least not to those looking for signs. The day before her wedding, Victoria sat in her bedroom, her hair being brushed by a maid. According to Roberts, the maid heard an owl knock against the window of the home three times in a vain attempt to enter; while Victoria thought nothing of the strange occurrence, her maid saw it as an omen, a portent of death.

The wedding came and went with nary a disruption. The reception was held in the Stoney home, in a magnificent ballroom. When the newlywed couple took the floor, all agreed that they made the loveliest couple. Those who congratulated the couple on their union, though, noticed how flushed the blushing bride was, how ill she looked. Someone might normally have said something, but under the circumstances, most attributed her complexion to excitement over the wedding. It wasn't until Victoria collapsed that guests and family realized what was happening. She was carried up to her bedroom to be seen by a doctor. He diagnosed her with what he called country fever and, with a heavy heart, informed the Stoneys and Baynard that there was little he could do. Already, Victoria was delirious with the fever, her mind's grip on reality as tenuous as her body's grip on life. By morning, with her husband weeping at her side, Victoria had slipped quietly into the great unknown.

Baynard, determined to memorialize his wife, called for the immediate construction of a mausoleum. Workmen hurried to erect the structure. Upon its completion just days later, Victoria was placed within its cold, stone walls. Baynard watched as the doors were sealed, his heart heavy with grief. He turned away and walked to his carriage, the carriage that had, days earlier, carried him and his wife from the church to the reception. It was now dressed for death, black satin streamers trailing behind it. He spurred his horses on and the carriage tore down the path. When Baynard didn't return, the Stoneys began to worry, their fears only slightly alleviated by reports that his carriage had been seen racing across the South Carolina coastline. Then, one day, they received a letter, with word that Baynard had also contracted country fever. Baynard welcomed and embraced his death, knowing that soon, he would be reunited with his beloved. Baynard died shortly after and was buried next to his wife in the Baynard Mausoleum. On the day that Baynard's body was interred in the mausoleum, witnesses throughout the area reported seeing his phantom coach, with the ghost of Baynard in it, and hearing the pounding hooves of his horses, black satin streamers trailing behind them.

Today, Hilton Head Island is the home of over 27,500 residents and a summer destination for more than 1.5 million tourists. The Stoney-Baynard home is a ruin now, a mere shadow of its former splendor and glory. The devastation accompanying the Civil War led to the abandonment of homes and plantations. Grand mansions fell into disrepair and the Stoney-Baynard home was no exception. The ruins are joined by the foundations of two other buildings, one marks what was once a slave dwelling, while the other remains a mystery. And, standing in Zion Cemetery, is the

Baynard Mausoleum, still standing after all these years. To visit the mausoleum is to relive the past, to remember what took place so many years ago when the dreams of a family were swept away by the hand of death.

When the black carriage wends its way through Hilton Head it is the past come to life. People still see the ghostly carriage and the ghost of William Baynard. While visitors may come and go, William Baynard is here still, haunting the island as he is haunted by his past.

OKLAHOMA
The 101 Ranch

They say you can hear them at night, off Highway 177, on a wide-open stretch of prairie just south of Ponca City. Cowboys—crooning over the nocturnal din of the plains, over the crickets, bullfrogs and coyotes, drifting in on a wind from nowhere. Sometimes the song is a cowboy's waltz, with harmonica, piano and guitar lilting through a pleasant melody. On other occasions, people have heard traces of an old western ballad, where one man sings a haunting melody accompanied only by the strains of minor chords on an acoustic guitar. There are other voices as well, the sounds of distant laughter and clapping; some have heard dozens of voices raised in unison singing one of the classic range songs of all time: "Whoopee ti yi yo, git along, little doggies, It's your misfortune and none of my own."

The distant sounds of this mysterious hoedown have been heard for about half a century now. Motorists taking a rest stop, tarrying picnickers and hitchhikers stranded along 177 late at night have all reported hearing the sounds of an antiquated party countless times over the years, making the cowpunchers'

Ghostly echoes of the 101 Ranch Wild West Show are still heard.

celebration near Ponca City one of Oklahoma's most enduring mysteries.

A mystery, yes, but none of the Oklahomans in Kay County have much doubt as to the origin of this strange soiree, though many people might prefer to leave the matter unanswered after hearing the popular explanation from local Sooners. It is a story that defies the conventional wisdom of our age. Who are these revelers? They are ghosts.

And not just any ghosts. For the sounds of the hoedown are always heard in the same area, off Highway 177, just south of Ponca City, the exact location where the legendary 101 Ranch used to be.

Today, there is only a picnic area and a National Historic Landmark where the headquarters for the world-famous 101 Ranch Wild West Show used to be. Established in 1879 by Colonel George W. Miller, the 101 Ranch—getting its name from the sprawling 101,000 acres it was spread over—was an immense operation. At its peak, it contained a fully staffed school, general store, hotel, cafe, magazine, newspaper, smithy, dairy, meat-packing plant and oil refinery. Home to about 3000 American citizens, the 101 Ranch was one of the

biggest ranching outfits in the West. George Miller's three sons took over the ranch when the colonel passed away in 1903. It was under the management of his three sons that the 101 Ranch became famous across the country.

In 1900, Wild West Shows were big business. Pioneered by Buffalo Bill Cody during the late 1800s, by the turn of the century, they were immensely popular productions, selling out pavilions around the world. The Millers drew from the talented hands they had working for them and by 1905 put together what was considered to be the greatest Wild West show in the country. Its very first show was a roaring success, and the 101 Ranch Wild West Show maintained its popularity for over two decades, traveling across the United States and even across the Atlantic to Europe. They were good times for the Millers—money was coming in, everyone wanted to be in their production and their three-story white stucco ranch home, which they called the Whitehouse, became a meeting place for every colorful character that whirled a lasso in the state of Oklahoma.

The brothers' splendid ranch headquarters was almost always packed with the best showmen from all the Wild West shows proliferating across the state. Celebrities such as Pawnee Bill, Buck Jones and the cowboy-philosopher Will Rogers were regulars at the Whitehouse. It was said that every weekend, the sounds of merriment coming from the Miller ranch could be heard for miles around. Gathering around an enormous campfire, the revelers sang, danced and shared stories about their innumerable escapades on the ranches and stages across the country.

The good times lasted well into the 1920s. Adding silent movies to their arena of operations, the Millers' business got better year after year and by 1925, it seemed that things couldn't possibly get better for the 101 Ranch. But they could definitely get worse. In 1927, Joe, the eldest Miller brother, died of carbon monoxide poisoning; two years later, the middle son, Zack, was killed in a car accident. That left the youngest, George, to manage the entire ranch by himself, a task he may well have been up to if the onset of the Great Depression didn't ravage the family business. By 1931, the 101 Ranch was financially ruined. In 1932, the Whitehouse was torn down, the property was divided up and the parcels of land were auctioned off to prospective farmers.

The coming years brought a great many new developments throughout Oklahoma and the world, but those pioneer entertainers who entertained on horseback with gun and lasso were past their heyday. Wild West Shows became a thing of the past, and the men and women who starred in the expositions were growing old. One by one, they passed on. Will Rogers died in an airplane accident in 1935 in Point Barrow, Alaska. But it wasn't until 1952, when George Miller passed on in his Texas home, that the bizarre reports of an invisible party began circulating around Ponca City.

Lone motorists running errands out of town were the first to hear the sounds of revelry carrying on the prairie wind.

When word got out that something strange was afoot south of town, groups of teenagers began taking trips out on weekend evenings, hoping to hear the strains of cowboy music drift in from the darkness; many of them were not disappointed. Farmers, townsfolk, hitchhikers, curiosity-seekers, paranormal enthusiasts—the tale of the haunted ranch grew with each visitation until the entire state came to know of the phantom hoedown in Kay County. And the sounds are said to still continue today, jovial laughter and music coming from somewhere around where the Whitehouse once stood.

Indeed, the first and last great actors of the drama of the Wild West seem intent on continuing what now appears to be an ageless celebration. Who knows? Maybe in the spirit world they inhabit, the buffalo still roam over the Great Plains, the American Indians are fierce and free and the range is still open all the way from southern Texas to the cattle towns of Kansas. Or, maybe they're living in an eternal present where there are still throngs of people willing to pay good money and sit in a pavilion to watch them reenact the romance of a time when the West truly was wild. Whatever the case, the party that began almost 80 years ago continues, testament that not all ghosts are tortured moaning souls obsessed with the injustices of their earthly years.

4
Spirits
on the
Menu

ALASKA
The Red Onion Saloon

Skagway continues to survive by the force of its past. Standing as a model of a bygone age, the small town had its heyday when gold was discovered in the Yukon. It served as a launching point for gold speculators arriving on the Pacific. From Skagway, miners took either the Chilkoot or White Pass Trails to the Klondike gold fields, where, if all went according to plan, they struck it rich. The northbound traffic brought unprecedented numbers to the Alaska town. With only 700 residents in 1897, the population shot up to 20,000 shortly after gold was discovered. About a year later, after the Klondike Gold Rush had run its course, Skagway returned to humble numbers, settling with about 700 mountain dwellers.

Skagway's status as a gold rush boomtown endowed it with so much cultural cachet that it has remained one of America's most desirable tourist destinations. Today, as many as 10,000 visitors visit Skagway every day during the summer months. On most days from spring to fall, there are at least five cruise ships anchored off the historic town, bringing the local merchants a constant stream of enthusiastic tourists. Perhaps it's fitting that a transfer point for gold miners 100 years ago has become a tourist gold mine today, ensuring the survival of Skagway's 800 or so residents.

But the town's dramatic history has had more than an economic effect. The trials and traumas from the town's tumultuous past did not simply disappear after the gold rush ended. Riches were made and lost during Skagway's one manic year; many hapless fortune seekers realized that fortune had passed them by on the town's crude street corners. And then there were those who incurred more severe losses, such as the speculators who lost their lives in pursuit of the yellow metal. Given the intensity of the circumstances, it's not surprising that some emotional residue still remains in the former boomtown—emotional residue that manifests itself as ghosts.

The prevailing idea is that the ghosts of Skagway are dead men and women whose difficult lives caused them to haunt the sites of their suffering. Frequent sightings of these 19th-century manifestations occur in the famous Red Onion Saloon, which still stands today on the corner of Second and Broadway.

During its heyday, the Red Onion was one of the most lucrative businesses in town. Boasting a saloon on the ground floor and a brothel upstairs, the establishment provided its patrons with two of the most popular commodities on the American frontier: whiskey and women. The Red Onion opened for business in 1898, just as miners rushed into town. Thirsty clients were always packed shoulder to shoulder in front of the 19-foot mahogany bar. As they argued and drank, many of these men kept a careful eye on the dolls arranged behind the bartender. Every prostitute on the second floor had a doll representing her displayed behind the bar. If the doll was reclined, it meant that the woman was busy; if the doll was sitting upright, the woman was waiting for another client in the 10 x 10 confines of her private office.

Surprisingly enough, there is no reminder of the dissolute denizens that frequented the Red Onion's main floor during its frantic year of business. But upstairs, in the cramped prostitutes' quarters, visitors have reported numerous unsettling experiences.

For many years, people on the ground floor have heard footsteps moving at a brisk pace across the hallway upstairs

Skagway, Alaska, is apparently haunted by ghosts of the gold rush.

when no one was supposed to be up there. Whenever anyone investigated the source of these sounds, nothing was found except an emptiness punctuated by an abnormal chill and a disturbing sense that someone was there. The sounds of the footfalls have been more pronounced on different occasions. An employee of the Red Onion once called the police after hearing someone running across the second floor hallway. Police found nothing there when they arrived to investigate.

Others have seen the transparent image of a woman slowly making her way across the second floor. She carries a water pitcher in her hands, bending down to water plants that aren't there, before disappearing into thin air. People who have seen this apparition claim that the moment the woman vanishes, a strong flowery scent suddenly fills the air, as if a powerful perfume was sprayed around them.

These strange sights and sounds recur today in the Red Onion Saloon. No one, however, knows who the transparent woman is or whose footsteps continue to make their rounds on the building's top floor. Indeed, the spirits could be participants in any one of the countless little dramas that must have taken place in the bordello while it was in operation. A nameless prostitute who continues to care for nonexistent plants? A frightened client trying to get away without paying? The stories behind the Red Onion's spirits will probably remain locked away in the lost particulars of the building's history, finding expression only in the supernatural events that continue to occur in the old saloon.

Arizona
Big Nose Kate's Saloon

Walk into Big Nose Kate's Saloon. Order a drink from the bar. Sip the drink and know that Wyatt Earp, Doc Holliday and the Clantons all stood in that spot and picked their drinks up off the same bar. Ignore the automobiles and the click and whir of cameras, and the Tombstone of old comes into focus with a clarity stunning in both its precision and detail.

Past, present and future converge in Big Nose Kate's Saloon. Its name hearkens back to a different time. Silver fueled Tombstone's creation and attracted men like the Clantons and the Earps with its promises of wealth. In the early 1880s, Tombstone was larger than Tuscon, but falling silver prices had crippled its growth by 1886. Few believed that Tombstone would survive, but it did, persevering through the Great Depression and the loss of its Cochise County seat to Bisbee. In 1962, Tombstone was named a Registered Historic Landmark. For a town of such historical richness, its past is the key to its future. Tombstone, "the town too tough to die," loves its history. Tourists now sustain the city, drawn by Tombstone's rich and visible past.

Every effort to preserve, recreate and restore the past has been made. The Boothill Gunslingers reenact the gunfight at the OK Corral daily, frequently to sold-out crowds. The Bird Cage Theatre on Allen Street was built in the 1880s and still stands, looking much as it did when its doors first opened and Wyatt Earp ambled in and found his third wife. Establishments such as Big Nose Kate's Saloon bear the names of long-departed celebrated residents.

Tombstone came into existence in 1879 when silver was discovered in the San Pedro Hills and Ed Schieffelin, the city's founder, named his discovery Tombstone. In March 1880, the first railroad from Tuscon to Tombstone was completed, and the town grew rapidly to a population of 6000. Men flocked to Tombstone to make their fortunes in the silver mines. But the work was long and hard, with few attaining the wealth they had envisioned.

Women also came to Tombstone seeking their fortunes. Those who wanted more than the lowly wages paid to seamstresses, cooks or laundresses worked in the saloons. It was a job fraught with peril but could be lucrative—women set their prices, and many of them made more money than those they serviced.

The first woman to open her own saloon was Big Nose Kate. Her real name was Mary Katherine Haroney, but she'd acquired the nickname on account of both her nose and her nosiness. Her fame was acquired through her association with two of Tombstone's most celebrated residents, Wyatt Earp and Doc Holliday. Although she denied it, many speculated that she and Earp had had an affair long before she ever met Holliday. Regardless, her name will now and forever be tied with Holliday. And, as it is with so many of the great love stories, theirs was a tumultuous relationship, passionate and manic. The pair fought and loved madly.

While she saved Holliday from the gallows at least once, she also was responsible for his arrest. After a stagecoach was robbed in 1881, Kate, drunk and enraged with Holliday after another of their epic fights, signed an affidavit stating that Holliday was one of the parties involved in the robbery. He was arrested and was released only when Kate recovered enough of her sobriety to recant her testimony.

Kate is immortalized today in Tombstone by the saloon that bears her name. She never owned this establishment; in fact, the saloon was once known as the Grand Hotel, home to

Tombstone's famed residents. The Grand Hotel attracted men like the Earps, the Clantons and the Mclaurys, and the hotel's register shows the latter two were registered as guests the night before the OK Corral gunfight.

As is the case with several other buildings, the basement of this saloon contains the remains of a mine shaft entrance. In its heyday, the Grand Hotel's bar was located here to serve thirsty miners who would emerge from the darkness for a quick drink before heading back to work. The basement was also home to a permanent resident, known now only as the Swamper, a janitor and handyman of sorts. His accommodations were paid for as part of his salary, but from his room in the Grand Hotel, the Swamper sought to augment his income.

Knowing that he slept just feet away from veins of silver ore, from the promise of untold riches, the Swamper set about creating his own private mine. Between his shifts at the Grand Hotel, the Swamper tunneled an entrance into the shaft. Ounce by ounce, the Swamper removed nuggets of silver. Nobody knows what he did with his lode, and there are whispers that his bounty is hidden somewhere in or around the saloon. Yet while the fate of his wealth is unknown, those in Tombstone know that the Swamper is still alive and well, at least in spirit.

The past comes to life literally in Big Nose Kate's. Visitors and staff have reported seeing a ghost roaming the halls and stairways of the saloon. Ghost hunters have caught the apparition on film, some in vivid detail. In 2000, Bill Samuels was on his way from California to work in Pennsylvania for the summer. A fan of westerns and ghosts, he decided a stop in Tombstone would satisfy both his passions. He had heard the stories about this town where almost every building experiences something unusual, from swinging chandeliers and phantom footsteps to flickering lights. He took many pictures that day, but said later, "we didn't find a whole lot of interesting things in most of these pictures." At least not until he looked at the photographs from Big Nose Kate's. "The picture we shot inside of Big Nose Kate's Saloon," said Samuels, "was astounding."

Inside the saloon is a steel cutout of a cowboy, his gaze fixed upon the bar, gun drawn in his left hand. Samuels took a photo of this display, but when the image was developed, he was astonished by what he saw. The lower half of the cowboy appeared blue, and the entire cutout was suddenly transparent, a quality steel does not possess. Eeriest of all was the face of the cowboy. Samuels described it as a "face with a mustache, well-defined nose and evil eyes." The only problem is that the face in the photo does not exist. It was not visible to anyone when the picture was taken.

To make sure that nothing had been missed, Samuels sent the photograph to the saloon's owner. "Several weeks passed," Samuels said. "I finally got the photo back with a note from the owner stating it was the weirdest picture he had ever seen to date." Numerous pictures had been taken of the steel cowboy over the years, but none had captured this phantom face before. For Samuels, the trip to Big Nose Kate's Saloon was a success. "I would brave the hottest Arizona summer or the coldest Arizona winter to take another like this one," said Samuels. "It is perhaps one of the best pictures of a ghost ever taken." But who is the strange cowboy? Could it be the Swamper?

The Swamper, locals believe, is still here to guard the silver he spent a lifetime accumulating, the silver that breathed life into Tombstone, that fostered the past upon which Tombstone now stands proudly and firmly.

NEW MEXICO
La Posada Hotel

Fortune was not kind to Julia Schuster, whose life changed the moment she caught the eye of Abraham Staab, a Santa Fe magnate visiting his German homeland on a nuptial quest. In the 19th century, the rules of courtship were different than they are today. The worth of a woman would be measured by the stature of her husband, and Abraham Staab was a powerful millionaire who made sure he got what he wanted. Julia really didn't have much of a choice; an offer of marriage from a man as powerful as Staab was not to be turned down. Shortly after she was wed, Julia moved back to Santa Fe with her new husband.

It was 1876, a time when the New Mexico town was on the peripheries of civilization. Julia spent the remainder of her life there, far away from her homeland and everyone she loved, contending with one heart-rending difficulty after another until death claimed her in 1896. She spent her final years dying a slow and painful death, ensconced within the luxurious space of her bedroom in the Staab Mansion, a true victim of the genteel mores she was taught to live by.

Abraham could not know he was commissioning the construction of his wife's tomb when he ordered work to begin on the opulent three-story Staab Mansion in 1884. Making sure he made up in material splendor everything he lacked in emotional depth, Abraham insisted the house be made into one of the most magnificent living spaces in Santa Fe. The Victorian-era mansion was filled with every luxury that money could buy, and Abraham and his wife entertained the socialites of New Mexico at some of the finest parties in the southwest.

La Posada de Santa Fe today

But a debilitating unhappiness rested underneath the velvet veneer of Victorian opulence. Abraham Staab was a hard man, whose connection with his family rested primarily on incessant, often vicious demands that he get his way. He insisted that his wife act according to his perceptions of propriety, that he should have as many children as he wished and that all his children fulfill familial obligations, meaning unconditional obedience to their father. For Julia, who would give birth to four boys and four girls while she was married, this meant decades of ceaseless work and emotional isolation. Expected to maintain an image of upper-class gentility, Julia learned to keep her complaints to herself, languishing in her own loneliness until a deep sadness settled on her soul.

Yet it was after one of her sons died in infancy that something inside Julia snapped. Not long after that, she fell victim to what history describes as a "dreadful accident," emerging with an unnamed physical disability that kept her confined to her bedroom. An invalid for the rest of her life, she spent the remainder of her days festering in an ugly depression, seen by none, not even her husband, until she died in 1896. While it is widely accepted that she died of illness, many have whispered rumors of homicide, and there has been more than one story of Abraham Staab stealing into Julia's room while she was sleeping to smother her with a pillow or shoot her with a pistol.

Many state that such rumors grew from the imaginations of those community members who tend to assume the worst, that Abraham Staab went through great pains to assure his wife got the best medical treatment and would have never committed such an act. Whatever the case, as meek as Julia Staab was when she was alive, suffering so many years of physical and emotional pain in stoic silence, subsequent events at the Staab Mansion suggest that she has not crossed over to the afterlife with the same docility.

In 1934, years after both Julia and Abraham had passed away, R.H. and Eulalia Nason, a wealthy couple from the Midwest, moved to Santa Fe on the recommendation of their doctor, who swore by the health benefits of the New Mexico climate. The Nasons were bewitched by the local culture and joined the Pueblo Revival Movement shortly after they purchased the Staab property. It was under their auspices that the current La Posada Resort and Spa was established. The adobes built around the Victorian mansion were eventually used as the lavish suites on the sprawling grounds of the luxurious resort that anyone can visit in Santa Fe today.

The Staab Mansion still stands in the center of the resort, housing a restaurant, bar and a number of ornate suites on the second floor. And it is there, in room 256, that the ghost of Julia Staab is believed to reside. It is the same room where she spent the last years of her life suffering in a solitary bedridden misery. Guests have reported waking in the middle of the night to see a well-dressed, slightly transparent woman standing over their beds or walking about the room randomly moving their belongings about. Whenever this woman is addressed, she vanishes into thin air before their eyes.

Other guests in room 256 have come back to their rooms after a day of sightseeing in Santa Fe to find their belongings rearranged. Suitcases that were open were found closed, toiletries that were in the bathroom were found arranged meticulously atop the nightstand in the bedroom, towels previously folded on towel racks were spread over the floor in careful patterns.

There is also the time Julia turned up the heat during one of Santa Fe's cold spells. It happened one evening when the temperature in Santa Fe had suddenly and unexpectedly dropped, leaving the residents in La Posada shivering in their rooms. The story goes that the only person who had the key to operate the thermostat had gone fishing, and the clerk at the front desk was being flooded with calls about the cold in the rooms. Sometime between seven and eight o'clock a call came in from room 256. A woman with a thick German accent told the clerk what he had already heard a dozen times that evening, except for adding the statement that *her* guests were all half-frozen. When he answered the best he could do was provide some blankets and hot beverages until the maintenance man with the thermostat key arrived, he received a brisk response. "Neveer, mind, I vill take care of eet myself."

Abraham Staab, builder of the Staab Mansion, the house that is the heart of La Posada de Santa Fe

Moments later, the heater was working, and within the hour the hotel was a comfortable room temperature. The desk clerk finished his shift without giving much thought to the heater, assuming that the maintenance man had returned and turned it back on. The clerk ran into the caretaker on his way out of the hotel and thanked him for turning the heat on. "Pardon me?" the caretaker replied, "I just got back in now. I didn't turn the heat on."

The strange call from room 256 instantly replayed itself in the clerk's mind. What did she mean by "her guests" being half-frozen? And he didn't recall anyone staying in room 256 having a German accent.

Julia continues to haunt La Posada today, appearing repeatedly to guests staying in room 256. She has also been spotted drifting down the second floor hallway, a pale woman dressed in 19th-century finery. She keeps a careful eye on the guests in her home, doing everything she can to ensure that guests in La Posada are enjoying their stay.

MINNESOTA
Forepaugh's Restaurant

Romance has a way of finding its way onto the menu at Forepaugh's, an upscale French restaurant in the resurgent neighborhood of Irvine Park in St. Paul, Minnesota. It is considered one of the most romantic restaurants in the city, revered for both its atmosphere and its cuisine. It seems as if it were always so, as if this mansion were always the setting for love, or, at the very least, for lust. And while romance is often idealized and stylized, rarely is it so picturesque or idyllic in practice. Love can turn ugly when the highs of ecstasy have faded and yielded to the lows of reality. Here, then, is the arc along which Joseph Forepaugh traced his path. In doing so, he contributed to a legacy that makes its presence felt even today.

Forepaugh's was named for Joseph Lybrandt Forepaugh, a senior partner in the firm of J.L. Forepaugh & Company. Forepaugh had found great success in establishing the first exclusively wholesale dry goods house in the state and the largest in the Northwest. In 1870, he acquired five lots in the Irvine Park neighborhood, whose residents included important figures such as Alexander Ramsey, Minnesota's first territorial governor. Constructed and centered upon these lots was the Forepaugh mansion, a glorious Victorian-style tribute to wealth. The structure was surrounded on all sides by manicured lawns and gardens and was decorated within with the finest furnishings Forepaugh could find. The grandest display, of course, was the Forepaugh family itself. With its self-made patriarch, doting wife and two beautiful daughters, the Forepaughs were the very picture of the American Dream, and their home, its architectural embodiment. Of

Staff at Forepaugh's Restaurant are kept busy with customers and ghosts.

course, dreams are rooted not in reality but in fantasy. All was not right in the Forepaugh home.

The family lived in the home for 16 years until abruptly departing for Europe, their mansion sold to General John Henry Hammond. Their departure aroused curiosity, for not long before they left, one of the Forepaugh servants, a young maid named Molly, had hanged herself in a third-floor bedroom. While the Forepaughs sought to keep the suicide a secret, pedestrians walking by the home had seen Molly twisting and turning, displayed as she was behind the third-floor bedroom window. Molly's death was undeniably public knowledge. People all found themselves preoccupied with one question. Why did Molly kill herself?

The Forepaughs may have escaped the prying eyes and the whispered suspicions, but they could not escape the truth. Forepaugh had visited despair upon his young servant. The two of them had fallen in love, but when Forepaugh learned Molly was pregnant, he abandoned her and told her to leave his home. Understandably, Forepaugh could smell scandal and was desperate to avoid its taint. He distanced himself from the servant, refusing to listen to her pleas. Desperate, confused and alone, Molly spoke out in the only way she could. Her suicide was the only way to stain Forepaugh's silence.

The Forepaughs returned to Minnesota in 1889. They returned to St. Paul and built a new home at 302 Summit Avenue, a perch from where they could look down upon both the city and their old home. Three years later, on July 8, 1892, Forepaugh took a walk to Irvine Park, put a gun to his head and shot himself dead. Forepaugh, so cavalier and careless in his treatment of Molly, met her fate, plagued, as she had been, by an overwhelming depression from which the only escape could be death. It's said that Forepaugh had convinced himself that his finances were crumbling, but when lawyers analyzed Forepaugh's estate upon his death, they found that his finances were in good shape. In addition to his numerous real estate holdings, he had $500,000 in other assets, a monstrous sum at the time. Perhaps Forepaugh's suicide was motivated not by greed but by the haunting memory of a young girl named Molly.

The original Forepaugh homestead went through a succession of owners and the housing and redevelopment authority finally took ownership and closed its doors. The fortunes of Irvine Park had turned; once an exclusive residential neighborhood, it had fallen far from grace. The house remained unoccupied until 1974 when Naegle Restaurants No Limit, Inc. purchased the property and began renovations to turn the once-stately manor into a restaurant.

Workers began to notice strange activity throughout the house. Matt Bertz, writing for *Downtown Key Magazine*, reported that pipes and electrical systems began malfunctioning mere days after their installation. But while unexplained phenomena were occurring all over the home, the strange activities were concentrated in a third-floor bedroom, the site of Molly's death and what is now Forepaugh's Sibley Room. Inside, workers could not explain why they always felt a draft, even when the room's doors and windows were tightly shut. Even now, patrons and staff will wonder why the scent of perfume is so strong and why extinguished candles will reignite even when the Sibley Room is empty.

Joan Frantz, an employee at Forepaugh's who was interviewed by Bertz in 1999, heard a loud banging coming from behind a ground-level storage closet, but when she opened it, she found herself staring at emptiness. Another time, she was applying lipstick in front of a first-floor mirror when she heard a strange rattling coming from the coatroom. She went into the room and realized that the coat hangers were shaking and rattling loudly, even though she was the only person in the room. Over the 13 years Frantz has worked in the restaurant, she has seen stacks of plates shake on their own and walked away from a set table only to return to it moments later to discover all the settings disturbed.

Molly is still here in the restaurant that now bears the name of the man who abandoned her. Some customers request to sit in the Sibley Room in the hopes of catching a glimpse of its permanent guest. For her part, Molly seems to bear the living no ill will. She has embraced her lot in the afterlife and seems to enjoy teasing patrons and staff, to let them know that they are not alone. She must relish the irony that she is now the permanent inhabitant of a home she was asked, so many years ago, to leave.

Missouri
Lemp Mansion

Its rise was meteoric; so too was its crash. Within the span of a generation, a family fortune was built and lost, leaving in its wake unanswered questions and a haunted stately home.

John Adam Lemp arrived in St. Louis from his home of Eschwege, Germany, in 1838. Initially, little distinguished him from the thousands of other immigrants who flocked to the Midwest in the 19th century to pursue their dreams. It wasn't long, however, before Lemp found himself rising above the masses to succeed where so many others had failed.

Lemp opened a grocery store that became quite popular. Oddly enough, its success had little to do with the freshness or quality of his products. The people of St. Louis flocked to Lemp's business for a new product few had ever had the opportunity to experience—lager beer. Having learned the art of brewing from his father in Eschwege, Lemp discovered that the natural cave systems under St. Louis provided the perfect conditions in which to brew his particular brand of homemade beer.

Before long, Lemp realized that he was in the wrong business. He closed his grocery store and created the Western Brewing Company. Before his death in 1862, Lemp amassed a small fortune for himself and his family. The lager proved wildly popular and earned accolades when it won first place at the annual St. Louis Fair in 1858. To his son, William, Lemp left one of the largest brewing companies in Missouri.

William immediately expanded the brewery's operation. He acquired a five-block area and erected a complex of Italian Renaissance buildings to accommodate the growing demand. By the middle of the 1890s, Lemp Lager was known across the country. The brewery became the first in the United States to establish coast-to-coast distribution of its product. What had started as a small family recipe had become a nationwide success.

William watched over the company closely, overseeing all its operations. To facilitate his work, he bought a home built by Jacob Fiekert in 1876. He immediately expanded and renovated the Italian-style mansion for use as both a residence and an auxiliary brewery office. Sitting at 3322 DeMenil, the Lemp mansion was a display of wealth and opulence, with each of its 33 rooms boasting various artifacts and paintings. Underneath it, a vast network of walkways and rooms was built into the city's system of subterranean caves. As a dedication to his father's work, William built a quarried tunnel that led all the way to the brewery.

The Lemp empire was at its peak, but it soon began to crumble. The early 20th century brought a mystifying run of misfortune that would claim the lives of five members of the Lemp family and see the end of the family business.

In 1901, William was devastated when the oldest of his children, Frederick, died suddenly of heart failure at the age of 28. The death sent William spiraling into a depression from which he would never recover. Acquaintances and employees noticed that William's attention to detail at work and at home suffered; they worried that their friend and employer had been overtaken by a crippling lethargy. The passing of a close friend, Frederick Pabst of the famous Milwaukee brewing company, hastened William's decline. The day before Valentine's Day in 1904, William retired to his bedroom, telling a servant that he wasn't feeling well. One single gunshot rang out from behind the bedroom door. William had shot himself in the head. He was survived by four children William Jr., Charles, Edwin and Elsa. With her inheritance, Elsa was considered the wealthiest heiress in St. Louis.

There was little question who would take over operation of the company. Charles was more interested in real estate, while Edwin was content to take his fortune and live the life of a recluse on a private estate. William Jr., assumed control. He faced a world far different than the one that his grandfather had left behind. In 1906, nine larger breweries joined to form the Independent Breweries Company, which created stiff competition for the now-dwarfed Western Brewery. The First World War devastated a number of companies throughout the United States, the Western Brewery Company included. William Jr.'s less-than-adequate stewardship of the company further compounded the problems. The implementation of Prohibition in 1920 was the death knell for the brewery.

1920 also bore witness to another Lemp family tragedy. Trapped in a loveless marriage, Elsa shot herself in her bedroom. While some believed that she had been murdered by her estranged husband, no charges were ever laid by the surviving Lemps. William followed his father into an all-consuming depression.

In 1922, he decided to liquidate his company's assets, closing its doors for good without warning. The company's 10-block complex, once valued at $7 million, was sold to the International Shoe Company for the paltry sum of $588,500. Shortly after, William Jr.'s behavior became increasingly erratic and nervous. Four days after Christmas 1922, he shot himself in the chest. The sun had, for all intents and purposes, set on the Lemp empire. It had risen and fallen in the space of one generation. Misfortune, however, continued to plague the surviving Lemps.

Charles took possession of the mansion, getting rid of its offices. He moved in with two servants, but really lived alone in the 33-room home. As the years passed, he grew more eccentric, more attached to the home. He wouldn't be seen in public for days on end and wandered the home's empty halls clad in gloves, frantic to avoid any contact with bacteria. Edwin, desperate to help, urged his brother to sell the mansion. Charles refused. In May 1949, he committed suicide; Edwin found the body.

The last surviving Lemp refused to take possession of the family home. Instead, Edwin retreated to his estate, content to entertain his friends in privacy. He died of natural causes in 1970 at the age of 90. His will demanded the destruction of all Lemp possessions—family papers, artifacts and paintings. The last of the Lemps was laid to rest at the family plot in Bellefontaine Cemetery. Nothing commemorates their lives except tombstones and a haunted mansion.

Abandoned by Edwin, the Lemp property became a boarding house. Its grandeur was quickly forgotten as the neighborhood, once fashionable, succumbed to urban decay. The home stood empty for weeks at a time, as residents rarely stayed for longer than a couple of days. It seemed that the tenants didn't enjoy being awakened in the evening by knocks on their doors or the sounds of footsteps in their rooms late at night. Tenants didn't like the home because it was haunted. No one was ever at their doors when they answered them, and when they were awakened by the sound of footsteps in their bedrooms, they never saw anything or anyone moving around their rooms. And so it was with the Lemp mansion until 1975, when Dick Pointer bought the home with intentions of opening a restaurant and inn.

Extensive renovations and repairs needed to be made to the 107-year-old structure, and the work took far longer than necessary. Pointer had trouble handling his contractors and workers, some of whom flatly refused to enter the mansion.

Working inside, some could never rid themselves of the sensation that they were being watched. Others were perturbed to see objects move of their own accord and grew tired of a worksite where tools disappeared overnight. The strange events didn't stop when the restaurant opened. Both customers and employees have seen glasses lifting themselves off countertops while a piano played itself and a pitcher of water swirled as if stirred by an unseen hand. The activity earned the restaurant a place on *LIFE* magazine's 1980 list of the most haunted places in America.

It's not known how many spirits haunt the restaurant, but with so many recorded deaths it's not unreasonable to assume that many are the spirits of the Lemp family. One can only hope that in death they found the peace and happiness that was denied to them in life.

NEW HAMPSHIRE
The Country Tavern

Captain Ford was tired, hungry and badly in need of a shave. Having spent 11 months at sea, he was glad to finally be home, away from the close company of his crew and the rolling deck of his ship. After bouncing along a rough road for a few hours, the captain caught sight of his stone house in the New Hampshire countryside. He was overwhelmed. The house was one of the newest buildings in the region; Ford had commissioned it to be built about a year before, just after he had married Elizabeth, the pride of Dunstable. Captain Ford's wife was a stunning young woman. She stood tall, with long dark hair that fell to her waist and a delicate face that cast a gentle light all about her.

Thoughts of Elizabeth kept Ford going during the long months at sea. The couple had been wed for only two months before his shipping duties called him out to the briny Atlantic for the better part of a year. He had missed her dearly, and now, as his home came into view, his heart began to pound in excitement at the thought of holding Elizabeth in his arms once more. An irrepressible smile was on his face as he opened the door to his home.

The sight that greeted him was unlike anything he could have imagined. Elizabeth stood by the hearth, obviously startled at his sudden appearance. The smile quickly dropped from Ford's face when he saw that Elizabeth was making the greatest effort not to appear terrified—a very real fear was burning not too far beneath the surface. Instantly, Captain Ford knew something was wrong.

That was when he noticed the bundle his wife was holding in her arms. It was an infant child, swaddled in a blanket, gurgling happily. Ford was dumbstruck for a moment, all at once counting the months he was absent, wrestling with the brutal implications of the baby and registering the look of guilt in his wife's eyes. Since he had been gone for nearly a year, there was no way this child was his. Ford could only get out one choked word: "Whose?"

Elizabeth pleaded, "Please, don't."

Something horrible happened to Captain Ford in the seconds it took for Elizabeth to beg for mercy. He gave himself up to the worst kind of rage. It would be best to leave the horrific details of what transpired next unspoken; it suffices to say that Ford's reaction to his wife's infidelity was unspeakably cruel. Where a young mother stood with her happy child only minutes before, now lay a dead newborn and a screaming woman slumped on her knees over her baby. Blood stained the walls, floor and furniture.

Ford wasn't finished. Grabbing Elizabeth by the hair, he dragged her upstairs, threw her into a closet and locked the door. Elizabeth's muffled screams filled the house as Ford lumbered down the stairs, took the child outside and buried it under a tree next to the house. When he came back in, Elizabeth was still screaming.

Ford interrogated her relentlessly for the next three days, sitting on the floor against the closet door, demanding to know the identity of the father. But the only response from within the closet was an occasional low whimper, the mournful sound of a woman who had just lost her child. Whether she had gone catatonic or decided to remain loyal to her anonymous paramour can never be known, but Elizabeth did not utter a word to her husband, even as he threatened her with unspeakable torture. When it became apparent that Elizabeth wasn't going to give her lover up, Ford opened the closet door and bludgeoned his wife to death. He buried her behind the house, several yards from where the infant was hastily interred.

Although this calamitous sequence of events transpired hundreds of years ago, in 1741, the tragedy seems to have left a supernatural imprint in what is now called the Country Tavern in the southern New Hampshire town of Nashua. The captain disappeared after the murders, and the Ford home went up for sale. Stories of strange goings-on in the building began circulating shortly after the next owners moved in.

It was said that Elizabeth Ford was often seen at the window in the back of the house, staring blankly at the same tree her child was buried under. She appeared as beautiful as she was in life—tall with striking features and regal bearing. The only difference was that her dark hair had become as white as snow. She would stand there for a few seconds—occasionally lingering for a little longer—before vanishing into thin air.

Children seemed to have the best rapport with the wayward spirit. Over the years, many young residents of the house told their parents of a nice lady who played ball with them. Those parents who asked what the lady looked like would always receive the same description: a very pretty lady with white hair. As the years passed, strange tales from the Nashua house began to circulate. But it wasn't until several years ago, when the house was converted into a restaurant called the Country Tavern, that the ghost of Elizabeth became one of New Hampshire's most famous spirits.

It seems that Elizabeth has become more active since her old home was opened to the public. More than one patron of the Country Tavern has left the restaurant in the middle of a meal, startled by Elizabeth's supernatural hijinks. She has been known to lift cups off tables and toss them across the dining room, yank plates of food from under customers as they were eating and terrorize women in the ladies' restroom.

One of her favorite pranks involves lifting women's hair off their shoulders while they stand in front of the mirror. She has also been known to take patrons' personal possessions. Without fail, however, she returns them later to the bathroom counter.

This isn't to say that Elizabeth is a malicious spirit. Those who have seen her have said they've felt no trace of hostility. In fact, many felt a sense of peace as the smiling young woman with white hair stood in front of them.

No one knows for certain why Elizabeth continues to haunt the home in which she met such a dismal end. Some believe that her last days were so traumatic that her spirit wasn't able to cope with her death. She remains in the building, not knowing that her body expired so many years ago. Others say that she is searching for her baby, somehow unable to comprehend that the child is gone somewhere else. Can this be why she is always found staring at the tree her infant was buried under? We can only hope that Elizabeth is no longer suffering and that if she is looking for her child, she will soon find him or her.

Florida
The Biltmore Hotel

When George E. Merrick first decided to join hotel magnate John McEntee Bowman in constructing a grand resort, his goal was to cater to the hordes of people who were flocking to Florida to take advantage of the state's land boom. Merrick had already created the residential and affluent neighborhood of Coral Gables, laying down strict guidelines to make sure that this area of mansions, golf courses and country clubs would remain as pristine and beautiful as residents' wallets were thick. The hotel would be the culmination of his work, a place for the wealthy to relax and a center for sport and fashion. Prominent hotelier Bowman had erected hotels in Los Angeles, Atlanta and New York and brought all his expertise to bear in guiding Merrick's vision to fruition. Construction began in 1925. Ten months and $10 million later, Florida's Biltmore Hotel was open and ready for business. The hype surrounding its opening captivated the imaginations of people in the north, many of whom caught trains marked "Miami Biltmore Specials" to see for themselves the Biltmore's first steps into history.

Within months, the Biltmore could bask in the glow of its success and popularity; its address had become the most coveted and desired in all of Florida, with stars such as Ginger Rogers, Judy Garland and Bing Crosby vying with royalty including the Duke and Duchess of Windsor for accommodations at this American interpretation of the French Riviera. A steady schedule of galas, fashion and water shows from North America's largest swimming pool kept the public fascinated. Thousands gathered under the Biltmore's copper-plated Giralda Tower on a Sunday afternoon to take in sights

Apparitions from the time the building was a hospital continue to appear in the restored and luxurious Biltmore Hotel.

ranging from synchronized swimmers to bathing beauties to alligator wrestling. Yet, while the people watched, they little realized that they too had become a spectacle, for where money went, so too did avarice. There were those in the crowds observing, devising means to deprive the wealthy of their fortunes. One of these individuals was Edward Wilson.

Wilson saw in the restraints of Prohibition the opportunity to amass a fortune by selling alcohol and gambling. At the Biltmore, Wilson would be able to work with a steady and reliable clientele of wealthy customers. Wilson established his operations on the 13th and 14th floors of the hotel, creating a speakeasy and casino.

In 1928, he took on a partner, Thomas "Fatty" Walsh, a mobster who had relocated to Florida from New York City to escape suspicion regarding the disappearance of several men. The partnership, initially warm, soon chilled. In March 1929, with over 100 people gambling at the tables on the 13th floor, Wilson shot Walsh twice. Walsh died, but by the time police arrived to investigate, they found nothing but Walsh's dead body. The floor had been cleared of all tables and people. The police had no witnesses, no evidence and no suspects. And when rumors began that the Dade County District Attorney's Office had spirited Wilson out of the country to Cuba, reports that the police were involved somehow with the gambling operation were quick to follow. The theory gained more momentum in 1946 when Los Angeles police officers heard that the FBI had in their custody a man named Wilson who confessed to Walsh's death. The LAPD asked for records of the Florida police investigation but were told that none existed.

The Biltmore suffered little in the wake of the news of Walsh's murder. It continued to prosper, soldiering on through the Great Depression on the strength of its aquatic galas. But even the Biltmore could not remain immune from the affects of World War II. The War Department appropriated the hotel and converted it into a hospital, sealing its windows with concrete and covering its marble floors with linoleum. When the war was over, it became the site of the University of Miami's School of Medicine and remained a hospital until 1968.

In 1975, Coral Gables, under the Historic Monuments Act and Legacy of Parks, acquired ownership of its fabled building.

For nearly a decade the once grand Biltmore sat unoccupied. The only people who would draw near were those attracted by reports of strange lights moving their way through the abandoned floors. People began to believe that any number of spirits haunted the Biltmore, that it was clear Thomas "Fatty" Walsh and various patients who passed away in the building when it was the Army Air Forces Regional Hospital still had unfinished business from their times on earth.

Finally, in 1983, the city undertook the full restoration of the Biltmore, ripping up linoleum to expose the marbled floors and pulling down concrete from windows. After four years and $55 million, the Biltmore reopened on December 31, 1987. A multinational corporation led by Seaway Hotels took ownership in June 1992, leasing the building from Coral Gables and making several significant changes to the property.

But while the Biltmore has been restored, some things within have never needed upkeep or restoration. When the building lay empty and abandoned for nearly 10 years, people thought it might be haunted. Now, people know that it is.

Most of the activity in the Biltmore is concentrated on the 13th floor, where Walsh died. Walsh's spirit is allegedly quite light-hearted, writing "Boo!" on steamy bathroom mirrors, opening doors for bellhops and stopping elevators on the floor even when the button for the 13th floor was never pushed. He is mischievous, not malicious, and longs for company. Walsh, though, is not the only spirit here.

A woman staying in the hospital in 1999 reported seeing the figure of a young man in a hospital gown walking in her room. Joyce Elson Moore describes in *Haunt Hunter's Guide to Florida* how, during a séance recorded on audiotape, a psychic felt the presence of an old man with a cane. While in the room the psychics heard nothing unusual, but when the tape was played back, recorded sounds of tapping were heard. The

The Biltmore's "Al Capone Suite," afterlife home of gangster Fatty Walsh

sound was so loud that it almost drowned out the psychics' voices. Moore also recounts the time a group of enthusiasts explored the hotel with tape recorders; they, like the psychics, heard nothing while in the building. But when the tapes were played back, everyone heard heavy breathing and sighs that hadn't been heard in the hotel, echoes of the Biltmore's past.

The Biltmore is now a National Historic Landmark, conferred that distinction upon its 70th anniversary in 1996. Its architecture has been displayed in films such as *Bad Boys* and *The Specialist.* It is now one of the world's premier luxury resorts, but it is reportedly the world's largest haunted house and Florida's most haunted hotel, home still to a varied roster of guests who have made their stay at the Biltmore permanent.

NEW JERSEY
Murders in Morristown

Jimmy's Restaurant on 217 South Street in Morristown, New Jersey, does not look very much like a stereotypical haunted house. It isn't in a state of irreversible disrepair, no loose shutters clatter in the wind, no dead trees grow on its yard and its wall corners display no cobwebs. In fact, Jimmy's, a former colonial home converted into a restaurant, is actually quite presentable.

The restaurant is one of Morristown's finer dining establishments, offering quality fare to locals and tourists alike. But there is a trace of something sinister in the pleasant environment of the establishment's dining rooms. Patrons and employees have often been startled by the feeling of an ice-cold hand on the shoulder. Others have heard rapid footfalls coming from an area where no one stands. And then there are those nights when, just under the dining room music, a low, painful moan can be heard drifting through the restaurant's rooms. Although it is barely audible, it still sends shivers up the spines of those who are able to discern the mournful sound.

Originally built by colonial patriarch John Sayre in 1749, the house was passed down through the Sayre family without event until May 11,1833, when a gruesome tragedy turned the home into one of New Jersey's most infamous houses.

The depraved events that cast an ugly pallor on the family house rest on the back of one man, Antoine LeBlanc. LeBlanc had emigrated from the West Indies and had also lived in Germany. He came to America with hopes of making his fortune, planning to earn enough money to marry his true love, a highborn young German woman named Marie Smicht. But it became obvious to LeBlanc shortly after he arrived in New Jersey that things were not going according to plan. Finding work as a hired hand for the Sayre family, he was dismayed to discover that the meager pay he received for his labor barely covered his lodging. With his current income, he knew that he would never make enough money to return to Germany and win his true love's hand in marriage. To add insult to injury, his junior position in the household meant that he took orders from everyone, including young Phoebe, a housekeeper almost a decade his junior.

Quickly growing desperate, LeBlanc hatched an evil scheme to get the money he needed. If he couldn't earn the cash, he would steal it. On a dark, moonless spring evening, the Sayres' hired help turned on his employers. Surprising Samuel Sayre in the stables, he crushed the poor man's skull with a shovel. LeBlanc then made his way into the house and killed Mrs. Sayre and young Phoebe in their beds. Next, he packed away every precious family possession he could find and stole away into the night with a bag of misappropriated goods.

He did not make it far. The villagers quickly learned of the horrible crimes committed in the Sayre home and pursued the murderer. They eventually caught up with him in a roadside bar, where LeBlanc was resting over a mug of beer.

The swift and merciless trial was expedited with relish. After LeBlanc was hanged for the murders, two local doctors took his corpse across the street and conducted experiments on it, testing a contemporary theory connecting electrical currents to muscular impulses. By applying electrical charges to LeBlanc's brain, they reportedly got his mouth to smile and his eyes to roll around in their sockets. One legend involves the two physicians trying to resurrect the convict by electrocution; if this was truly their aim, they failed at creating a monster. Such disrespect for LeBlanc's corpse says a lot about the antipathy the locals felt for the murderer. The story, however, did not end there.

After the experiments were over, LeBlanc's corpse was skinned and his epidermis was sent to a local tannery, where all sorts of household items were made from the murderer's skin. The purses, book jackets, lampshades and wallets that were produced from LeBlanc's cured hide became hot items on the local market. Never was a man so hated in Morristown.

Years passed, and the tragedies at the Sayre House were gradually forgotten, eventually fading into local history. All that changed after 1946, when the Sayre House was remade into a restaurant. It was then that the strange things began to happen. Service staff heard harsh whispers close to their ears as they tried to take orders from customers. The words were never discernible, but they almost always startled the servers, who looked over to see nothing where the urgent hissing had come from. Inexplicable drafts frequently wafted through the restaurant; at closing time, more than one staff member refused to be left alone in the restaurant after hearing footfalls from invisible feet running across the second floor.

These occurrences continued until a fire ravaged the building in 1957. It was rebuilt as the Wedgewood Inn shortly after, but it quickly became apparent that the fire had not purged any of the spirits that resided there. The ghostly activity continued, even after the restaurant changed hands. Whether it was called the Society Hill Restaurant, Argyle's or Phoebe's, outlandish occurrences continued to be reported. Doors were seen opening and closing by themselves; lights would switch on and off, seemingly of their own accord; and employees became wary of the basement after one bartender saw a lit candle moving through the cellar with no one holding it.

When the restaurant was still called Phoebe's—named after the Sayres' slain housekeeper—several waitresses had eerie encounters with the mirror in what was once Phoebe's room. On numerous occasions, an entirely alien person appeared in the looking glass. She was a pale young woman with blonde hair who stared blankly out of the mirror. At the sight of this startling reflection, more than one waitress let a tray stacked with glasses crash to the floor.

Based on these sightings, it has been assumed that the spirit haunting Sayre House is that of Phoebe, the family's erstwhile servant. But some psychics who have investigated the building claim to have felt a virulent anger emanating from some of the rooms. They are of the opinion that innocent Phoebe, who was killed in her sleep, would not generate such powerful energy. In other words, the spirit is more likely that of Antoine LeBlanc. Perhaps he is still angry about his inability to return to Germany or the great distance between him and his beloved. It is also possible that his spirit is unable to move on, still furious at the disrespect the people of Morristown showed his remains.

Regardless of the ghostly activity, the owners of Jimmy's Restaurant continue to operate their establishment. If fact, the spirits in Sayre House seem to add something to a dining experience in the bistro, where customers are treated to a fine meal and an interesting slice of New Jersey's history.

ARKANSAS
Crescent Hotel

It's been a school for young women. It's been the home of a fraudulent doctor. It's been the sight of some of the strangest things ever witnessed. It is the "Queen of the Ozarks," the historic and haunted Crescent Hotel.

Built between 1884 and 1886 by architect Isaac L. Taylor, the Crescent Hotel has a colorful and vibrant history, marked by both fortune and misfortune. When it first opened, the Crescent Hotel brought a touch of opulence and grandeur to Eureka Springs. In turn, the hotel prospered through its proximity to the community's hot springs. Visitors flocked to the hotel to take advantage of its luxury and to bathe themselves in the hot springs, which were believed to cure a host of assorted ailments. The hotel proved so popular that Frisco Railroad, the company that first brought the train to Eureka Springs, acquired the property in 1902. But Frisco Railroad hadn't counted on the fickle nature of humans.

By the early 20th century, the curative powers of hot water springs had been called into question and the wealthy had decided that there were other things to spend their money on. A train ride to visit the popularly dubbed "Queen of the Ozarks" no longer held allure. Just five years after acquiring the hotel, the Frisco Railroad abandoned the Crescent. Its financial problems were simply too much to overcome. In 1908, the building became the home of the Crescent College and Conservatory for Young Women. It limped along financially until it was forced to close in 1924. The building stayed close for six years until another eager educator opened a junior college. That endeavor lasted just four years. The property continued to change hands for several years, with businesses coming and going in quick succession. Then, in 1937, Norman Baker came to Eureka Springs.

Baker arrived in Arkansas with millions of dollars. He had acquired his great wealth through the invention of the Calliophone, an organ played with air pressure, not steam. But organs were only a hobby for Baker. Baker's passion lay in medicine. With no training whatsoever, he claimed to have discovered a number of cures, only to have their use and application thwarted by the established medical profession. He was convinced that he was the target of a vast conspiracy, and in Eureka Springs he found the perfect venue from which to ply his trade. A previous attempt to run a health resort in Muscatine, Iowa, only resulted in his expulsion from the state. The American Medical Association took issue with Baker's lack of a medical license and his highly questionable cure for cancer (he called for patients to drink spring water). And so it was that Baker found himself in Eureka Springs.

He bought the Crescent Hotel and began advertising his miracle cure for cancer. When the cure failed, a number of his patients suspected that perhaps Baker really was ignorant about medicine. The state filed charges against him, and Baker, convicted of mail fraud, was sentenced to serve four years in Leavenworth. Once again, the Crescent Hotel was abandoned.

In 1949, people who still remembered the charm of the Queen of the Ozarks bought the property, determined to resurrect its moribund spirit and elevate the establishment to a semblance of its former prominence. The hotel reopened and began to reclaim its place in Ozark history. Soon enough, however, it became clear that one reason that the hotel had had such difficulty in the past was that it was undeniably haunted.

The Crescent Hotel is said to have a spirit for each of its four floors. On the first is the ghost of a middle-aged mustached man, dressed in Victorian formal wear. Appearing to guests in the lobby and bar, he vanishes the moment anyone attempts to communicate with him. On the second floor, in room 218, is the apparition of a man who has been with the Crescent Hotel from the day it opened. Appliances such as the television turn themselves on and off and guests are kept up through the night by loud poundings coming from within the room's thick walls or by the ghost shaking them from slumber. Room 218's ghost is that of a construction worker who fell off the roof during the Crescent Hotel's initial construction. He met his death on the floorboards of what would become room 218.

A number of witnesses in 1987 couldn't believe their eyes when, one evening, they saw a nurse on the third floor, pushing a gurney down the hallway and then disappearing into the wall. Guests on the fourth floor must contend with the lingering spirit of a young woman who is believed to have jumped off the upper balcony to her death. Doors open and close on their own and footsteps can be heard in the hallway.

One evening, according to an account given to *Lone Star Spirits*, a couple was watching television in their room. The husband thought he saw out of the corner of his eye something moving to his left. He assumed the clothes he had sloppily thrown on top of the dresser were falling to the floor. But then his wife "grabbed his arm...and [he] felt a cold chill run through [his] body." She told him to look in the open closet, and when he did, he understood what had frightened his wife so. A pair of her blue jeans, draped on a hanger, were floating in the air, as if "someone was grabbing them by the bottom and...holding them tightly horizontally from the hanger."

And roaming throughout the hotel is the ghost of the man who guided the Crescent Hotel through some of its more notorious days, Norman Baker. It seems as if the good doctor has returned once more to the scene of his downfall, perhaps still convinced that the hot springs in Eureka are the key to defeating cancer. He lurks in the lobby, at the foot of the stairway and has also been known to frequent the recreation room.

The Crescent Hotel's haunts have garnered it attention not seen since its days as a retreat in the late 19th century. The establishment was featured on NBC's *Unsolved Mysteries* and is reportedly one of the most haunted buildings in the state of Arkansas, a fact that the hotel's current owners do not shy away from. While there was initial reluctance to speak openly about the hotel's hauntings, that all changed when Marty and Elise Roenigk took ownership of the Crescent in May 1996. They both have made an effort to be more ghost friendly. After all, businesses come and businesses go, but it seems as if the spirits of the Crescent Hotel are here for the duration.

SOUTH DAKOTA
Villa Theresa Guest House

The Villa Theresa Guest House traces its roots back to 1891, when an entrepreneur named Fred T. Evans saw possibilities in a plot of land overlooking the warm mineral springs in the southwest corner of South Dakota. Around the turn of the century, immersion in sulfur-heated water from natural hot springs was considered a remedy for everything under the sun. Evans recognized the potential to profit from providing retreats for upper-class Americans in search of rural palliatives. He built the prototype for the Villa Theresa, the Sioux City Club, right next to the recently incorporated town of Hot Springs. The retreat served as an exclusive men's gaming club, where gentlemen roomed in opulent suites after full days of leisure.

Hot Springs grew during the first decades of the 20th century, and the Sioux City Club got the attention of a Chicago tycoon named F.O. Butler in 1916. Butler added to the existing structure, constructing most of what is now the Villa Theresa as an inn for his circle of affluent friends. Little is known about the type of revelries that took place in the villa, but Butler maintained proprietorship over the building throughout the 1920s, which were known for bacchanalian festivities of the urban elite.

It is likely that the parties affected some people deeply— so much so, in fact, that they would remain attached to the house after death. Although time marched on and the property changed hands more than once, some part of the grand home remained in the 1920s.

This is obvious to anyone who spends time in the Villa Theresa today. Currently serving as a luxurious bed and breakfast, the carefully preserved guesthouse has lost few of its bucolic charms—or even guests. It seems that some of the early revelers at the Villa Theresa are reluctant to abandon the idyllic ambience of their old vacation spot. Stories of unbidden and unfamiliar visitors wandering through the house have been in circulation for some time now, even before the house was made into a B & B.

Very few previous owners have felt comfortable in the old resort. Many semitransparent apparitions have been spotted on a winding staircase that ascends from the living room. Some have seen an elegant woman dressed in a luxurious old evening gown slowly descending the stairs. Her skin is said to be white as alabaster and her beautiful face completely expressionless. Those shocked observers who did not flee at the sight of this phantom visitor could only stare as she disappeared into thin air.

The house's spirits seem unnaturally drawn to the staircase, which connects the tower copula to the living room. The apparition of an older man dressed resplendently in early 20th-century finery has also been seen descending the winding staircase. Others have witnessed a disturbing display of domestic violence, in which two faint apparitions—one man, one woman—are locked in a struggle halfway up the stairs. This supernatural melee usually lasts only a few moments before both combatants vanish. People who have witnessed this struggle have claimed to feel a sudden rush of panicked energy, as if they too are part of the fight on the stairs. They report feeling wobbly legs, fluttering stomachs and sudden urges to strike something or run. But the moment these spirits disappear, the feelings of nervous energy dissipate into nothingness, leaving bewildered witnesses exhausted and confused by the bizarre events that just transpired.

Fewer reports of supernatural activity on the staircase have been made since the Villa Theresa was turned into a bed and breakfast. In other parts of the house, however, strange events have continued to transpire. Doors open and close by themselves. People awaken in the middle of the night to see orbs of light hovering over their beds. Other apparitions are seen drifting aimlessly through the halls of the house. One woman swore that she woke to find the apparition of F.O. Butler standing silently at the foot of her bed.

Why so many spirits continue to inhabit the Villa Theresa is unclear. It could be that early visitors had such memorable experiences that they were unwilling to leave the place after death. Or perhaps the building's proximity to the Black Hills, a region central to the spiritual mythology of the Sioux Indians, somehow led to the hauntings in the old house. All that can be said for certain is that visitors to the Villa Theresa continue to witness strange events to this day.

5
Haunted by History

OHIO
The Taft Museum

This story is a selection from Edrick Thay's Ghost Stories of Ohio.

She has a way of helping people believe.

Chief of Security at Taft Museum, John Ring, can still recall the moment he cast skepticism aside and began to believe. He told his story to Derek Krewedl of the newspaper *The Downtowner* in October 2001. Ring's moment of epiphany was in the late 1970s. He was watching over a chamber music concert when he was approached by several guests, each with the same complaint—they were distracted by the sound of a crying baby just in the background, somewhere outside the music room. Ring set off to investigate. But even after an exhaustive search of the building's other rooms and hallways, no baby was ever found. In fact, after questioning other employees about the incident, Ring learned that a baby hadn't even been in the building that day. He remembered that when he first began his job, he had been regaled with eerie stories by other security officers—stories of strange cries and footsteps in empty places.

But it wasn't until she entered the picture that Ring understood fully what he'd been told. As he was walking down the long hallway just outside the concert room, Ring heard footsteps behind him and then his name called out in a woman's voice. He turned around to respond but there was nothing there. She had called out to him, and he was converted. Annie had shown him the possibilities and now, every time Ring passes by her portrait in the Music Room, he is careful to wish Mrs. Taft a good morning.

Annie Taft died in 1931 and her home and its collection of art, so lovingly and painstakingly created over many years

The beautiful Taft Museum celebrates its many works of art—and the ghost of one of its former residents.

with her husband, passed to the people of Cincinnati. The house, built by merchant Martin Baum in 1820, now stands as the Taft Museum, and the Tafts' collections of European paintings and Chinese porcelains are displayed in it.

Baum constructed the large Federal-style house on a lot on the eastern edge of Cincinnati but didn't live there long, as the bank panic of 1820 devastated him financially and he was forced to move. The grand building was then used as an all-girls school until 1829, when it was bought by one of Cincinnati's wealthiest citizens, Nicholas Longworth. A patron of the arts, Longworth commissioned artist Robert Scott Duncanson to paint eight murals on the house's walls, works that launched Duncanson's career and established a legacy of arts support within the home that continued when David Sinton bought the home in 1871. While the murals are now seen as trademarks of the Taft home, the Tafts themselves never saw them. It wasn't until the home was being transformed into a museum that layers and layers of wallpaper were stripped away to reveal the stunning river and landscape scenes.

Sinton lived in the home with his daughter, Anna, and her husband, Charles Phelps Taft, the older half-brother of former President William Howard Taft and publisher of the *Cincinnati Times-Star*. The two were married in the upstairs Music Room in 1873, and when Anna's father died in 1890, her inheritance made her the richest woman in Ohio, a position allowing her and husband to pursue their love of the arts. Between 1902 and 1927, the two amassed what Jane Durrell called, on the 60th anniversary of the Taft Museum, a "coherent and harmonious collection, a first-class collection of art."

Charles passed away in 1929 and Anna in 1931. The house, along with its art collection, was willed to the city of Cincinnati. In death, the Tafts had established a means of passing on to generations the same pleasure they felt when they walked through their home, gazing upon their collected works of art. But it seems too that the Tafts themselves might also be enjoying their home and their life's work, even in death.

Staff maintain that there are a number of spirits roaming the halls of the Taft Museum. History has had time to foster the development of a number of spirits. David Sinton, his daughter and her husband all died in the home. It is the daughter, Anna, who is undoubtedly the best known spirit.

She is said to be a friendly, if mischievous, spirit, fond of interacting with staff and patrons. Owen Findsen, a reporter for the *Cincinnati Enquirer*, recorded an account by Chief of Security Ring on Halloween in 1995. Ring indicated that he was working in the garden when he noticed two ladies leaving the Taft Museum in a bit of a hurry. Apparently, the two ladies, mother and daughter, had been in the parlor looking at a painting. The mother claimed that someone had tapped on her shoulder, only when she turned, no one was there. The two decided to leave the place quickly. Anna's overtures were not accepted at that time.

Another time Anna appeared to a girl waiting for her boyfriend, a security guard at the museum, to come to the car. The girl waved at the figure standing at a second-floor window, thinking it was her boyfriend. The figure did not wave back. When the boyfriend finally finished his shift and got into the girl's car, she asked him why he hadn't waved back at her. He claimed that he had been in the basement and had not been upstairs at all. The second floor had been locked down; any movement there would have set off motion sensors.

In the gift shop, books will fall off shelves, only to land, every time, five feet away, face up. In a downstairs office with only one entrance, employees will return only to find that someone or something has wedged a chair underneath the doorknob, not outside, but inside the office. One time, several stacks of heavy books were placed in front of the door after it was locked; when morning came and people returned to work, they cleared away the books, only to find that their attempt to thwart the supernatural had failed. Upstairs, the attic has many unexplained cold spots, and more than one

The apparition of Anna Taft was spotted on the balcony of the museum that used to be her home.

worker has reported feeling that someone was blocking his or her way into an attic hallway. Who is responsible for all these events isn't exactly clear; it may be Anna or any of the other spirits in the Taft Museum. There are times, of course, when there can be no debate.

Even in death, Anna has not lost her passion for the artistic creations of man. Findsen recounted an afternoon when Anna herself made an appearance in spirit form. Katie Laur was in the garden playing country music when a gift shop customer, Treva Lambing, noticed that a security camera at the back of the museum seemed to be malfunctioning. Instead of panning across the grounds as it was supposed to do, the camera was pointing straight down at the ground. Lambing went over to make a report to a security guard on duty at the time. But when she reached the guard, Lambing noticed that she was staring up at the balcony. So she looked up too. And there, on the balcony was the figure of a woman in a long, pink gown, her feet tapping to the beat of the music. The way she looked, and the fact that there is no door to the balcony, convinced the onlookers that she was the spirit of Anna, taking time to enjoy the music in the sweet perfumed air of the garden.

Anna is such a presence here that Ring makes sure that all new employees meet and greet her portrait. This sort of initiation happened to Tamera Muente when she started working at the Taft Museum in late 2001. Despite the introduction, Muente, months later, "is still waiting patiently to meet Annie." She may have to wait awhile. The museum is currently closed, undergoing major renovations. The changes may very well drive away the spirit, but one should hope that Anna stays, for she is perhaps the most valuable specimen in a house full of priceless objects.

HAWAII
Queen Liliuokalani

The Hawaiian Islands are not often associated with political struggle, popular disenfranchisement and disgruntled spirits from the past. But there is much more to the Aloha State than pristine beaches and luxurious resorts. It once marked the front line where two cultures clashed, where the interests of American enterprise collided with the needs of a sophisticated indigenous population. In Hawaii's case, the interests of American businessmen won over the popular Hawaiian desire to maintain a monarchy independent of the United States. At the center of this struggle was a Hawaiian leader who struggled against the American sugar planters whose ultimate goal was American annexation.

Her name was Queen Lydia Liliuokalani, an intelligent woman whose regal bearing, political acumen and democratic sensibilities made her a powerful and effective voice for her people. But after a fierce political struggle against American capital, the queen abdicated her crown in 1893 to a business-friendly provisional government. The arrangement offended President Grover Cleveland's democratic sensibilities; he tried to reinstate Liliuokalani a year later but was opposed by a congressional vote. The queen's attempt to convince Congress of her people's cause in Washington did not succeed either. She ended up spending the rest of her days in Honolulu's Royal Palace, resisting depression and indolence by continuing to lobby for social reform and the poor. The last queen of the Hawaiian Islands passed away in 1917, a stalwart champion of her people to the end.

But that is not the end of her story. Some part of Liliuokalani seems to have survived her body's expiration.

Custodians working night shifts have long whispered among themselves about the queen's shadow drifting through the halls of the legislative building. Others report seeing a regal-looking woman adorned in a brilliant gown, whose austere features are softened by dark compassionate eyes. She seems to stare right at those she appears before, then slowly vanishes into the air.

Yet as difficult as Liliuokalani's earthly trials were, she is not an entirely melancholy spirit. On many occasions, Hawaiians have spotted her on the stairway in front of the capitol building holding bunches of leis with a broad smile on her face. Those who have seen her report being filled with an overwhelming sense of warmth and well-being. Many believe that her appearances occur more and more frequently and serve to spread joy to all Hawaiians fortunate enough to see her. Perhaps the previously forlorn spirit of Hawaii's first lady is becoming more contented as the years pass. But why has Liliuokalani grown serene? That is another question.

In 1982, the state erected a statue in the queen's honor on the grounds of the capitol. Some people believe this dedication to Liliuokalani's memory justifies her sacrifice and sorrow. Her newfound benevolence reflects a recognition that her work was not in vain. Others have claimed that the spirit of Queen Liliuokalani is pleased with the resurgence of Hawaiian pride since the early 1980s. After all, more Hawaiians today are fascinated by their roots than ever before, and Hawaii has never been studied so much in universities. With so many to reasons to celebrate, it's not surprising that the spiritual embodiment of the state is beaming.

WASHINGTON
The Ghost of Kickisomlo

It is one of the underlying themes of American history: that this immense nation is actually conquered territory. While it might be difficult to see it in the clamorous metropolises, the meticulously staked farms or carefully regulated park lands, there was a time in the not too distant past where there were no state boundaries, no highways, no cities, no common currency. We forget that in its early form, America was an alien land, a place where few modern Americans would even be able to survive. The transformation of the continent from what it was then to what it is today was a violent metamorphosis, where years of warfare between the first generations of American settlers and the American Indians made indigenous populations strangers in a land that was once theirs.

Chief Seattle of the Suquamish Indians in the Pacific Northwest was a peace-loving man who cooperated with the federal authorities every way he could. Seattle had no illusions about how desperate the situation was for his people. With full knowledge of what would happen to the Suquamish if they were to resist the flood of settlers to the west, he ceded vast tracts of wooded Washington to the United States. So it was that Seattle put the well-being of his people in the hands of a dominant American power, holding on to the hope that such collaboration might win favor with the conquering power.

Seattle, aware that he was the leader of a defeated people, was stoic in his grieving over the loss of the land and way of life. The days of the Suquamish were gone—this he knew—but Seattle was not completely crestfallen by the fall of his tribe. For he also knew that a legacy that ran as long and deep as that of the Suquamish could not, would not, simply vanish into nothing. He was certain that a land that had been integral to his people's culture would not let go of the Indian spirit so easily, that forever after, the country would be a haunted land, whispering to future generations of the ghosts of its past. In 1854, after signing a reservation treaty with Governor Isaac Stevens, Seattle gave a speech heavy with ominous prophecy:

And when the last Red Man shall have perished, and the memory of my tribe shall have become a myth among the White Men, these shores will swarm with the invisible dead of my tribe, and when your children's children think themselves alone in the field, the store, the shop, upon the highway, or in the silence of the pathless woods, they will not be alone. In all the earth there is no place dedicated to solitude. At night when the streets of your cities and villages are silent and you think them deserted, they will throng with the returning ghosts that once filled them and still love this beautiful land.

More than a century has passed since Chief Seattle delivered his famous speech, and considering the prominent place Indian spirits occupy in the canon of supernatural literature, the chief was not speaking idly. If one were to tally all the stories of wayward spirits suspected to be related to America's indigenous, a case could easily be made for the theory that the entire country is haunted by ghosts of the people who lived on this continent thousands of years before the United States was even formed. Hallowed ground, haunted burial sites, famous battlegrounds—does the very earth still belong to the American Indian, whose way of life no longer is? Many in the United States believe so.

The spirit of dignified Princess Angeline roams Seattle.

Of all these Indian ghosts, one of the most famous is none other than the daughter of Chief Seattle, Kickisomlo. Dubbed Princess Angeline by white settlers in the Northwest, the proud Suquamish woman lacked the riches of royalty but was in no short supply of dignity. She was born in 1820, living through the dissolution of the Puget Sound Indians, ending her days on the waterfront of Seattle, where she barely eked out a living as a laundress, depending on the charity of others to put a roof over her head. Though settlers originally bestowed princesshood half-mockingly, with time, everyone on the hard waterfront became convinced of Kickisomlo's royalty. It was the silent resilience with which she bore her poverty, the undeniable pride in her eyes as she went about the menial chores of her daily duties, her natural grace that set her apart from the teeming bustle that elevated her to royalty in so many people's eyes.

Kickisomlo passed on in 1890. She was buried in Lakeview Cemetery on Seattle's Capitol Hill, along with all her memories of a world gone and forgotten. But it soon became apparent that Kickisomlo herself was not going to simply disappear. Her likeness began appearing on postcards and souvenirs in gift shops all over Seattle shortly after she was interred. Photographs showed a prim old Indian woman staring into the camera with a mysterious look in her eyes. Princess Angeline was painted onto china, carved into spoons, placed on store advertisements. After she died, Kickisomlo truly did become Seattle royalty.

And true to her father's words, the dead princess was not eager to leave the land she knew when she was alive. Sightings of Princess Angeline began shortly after the Pike Place Market was established in 1907. Most people did not look twice at the elderly Indian lady walking through the crowded market with a shawl tied over her head and a cane in her hand. Yet those who did notice were struck by her resemblance to the woman who adorned so many pictures and keepsakes. The woman hobbled through the throng of shoppers, always taking the same route to the Craft Emporium, where she would suddenly disappear right in front of shocked witnesses.

Over the years, people fascinated with the story of the Indian apparition discovered that she appeared most frequently for one week every three months. While the meaning of these three-month intervals is largely a mystery, some have speculated that her walk through Pike Place marks the changing of the seasons. She may indeed be a harbinger of the seasonal changes in the yearly cycle, sensitive to the climatic patterns that shaped the lives of her people in Puget Sound.

It could be that this is her way of commemorating the Suquamish, keeping their legacy alive with her seasonal sojourns through the crowded walks of Pike Market. Or maybe she wanders Seattle streets in spite of herself, her soul as lost in death as it was in life, belonging to both her native tribe and the surging town that would become the city of Seattle. Either way, Princess Angeline is still seen today, making her way through the market crowds before disappearing in the beads section of the Craft Emporium, her continued appearance a reminder of what came before the business and bustle of modern America.

VIRGINIA
Edgar Allan Poe

If there was ever a perfect candidate to become a spirit, writer Edgar Allan Poe might just be the one. Fascinated both with the afterlife and the nature of death, Poe's obsessions found expression in the macabre, in his classic renderings of the American Gothic in "Fall of the House of Usher" and "The Raven." Interest in the spiritual came at to Poe an early age; already abandoned by his father, he was not quite three years old when his mother, Elizabeth Arnold Poe, died in Richmond, Virginia, from tuberculosis. While Edgar had been born in the cosmopolitan world that was Boston, it was in genteel Richmond that he found a home for both his heart and his weary soul. Care of Edgar fell to his godparents, the Allans, in Richmond. Poe took his adopted family's surname and an immortal triumvirate of names was born.

While the Allans did what they could for young Poe, he never completely recovered from the loss of his mother. He wrestled with depression throughout his life and was forever haunted by the specter of death and the afterlife. His spirit is said to be in Richmond still, haunting Talavera, a home he visited before his death.

The Allans shuttled in and out of homes around Richmond and then traveled to Europe where Edgar was educated in schools in England and Scotland. When they returned to Richmond, they settled in Moldavia, Poe's last home in Richmond, where he lived until he began studies at the University of Virginia. Across the street from the Allans lived the Roysters and their daughter, Elmira. A romance blossomed between the two youngsters, but any hopes for the budding romance were crushed under the weight of Elmira's

Edgar Allan Poe

parents' disapproval of Poe. Poe never forgot Elmira and it was to her he would later return.

Soon after entering the University of Virginia, Poe left both the university and the state. Though he had shown an aptitude in the classical and romance languages at university, he left school after a quarrel about his gambling debts with his adoptive father, John Allan. Poe headed north to the city of his birth, Boston. Without support from his wealthy parents and with no steady income of his own, Poe soon fell into poverty and was forced to join the army. While enlisted, he completed work on a volume of verse he had begun while in

Richmond. Published in 1827, *Tamerlane and Other Poems* chronicled his split from the Allans.

Poe did reconcile with John Allan, albeit half-heartedly, as a favor to his dying adoptive mother. With the reconciliation and subsequent financial support, Poe was able to leave the army. He was granted an honorable discharge and soon after, resumed studies at West Point. Allan's remarriage, though, severed any support Poe might once have had. Without his father's influence to lobby on his behalf, Edgar was expelled from West Point for numerous infractions.

In 1829 and 1831, Poe offered two more volumes of poetry. None of these three volumes garnered much attention or acclaim, and a defeated Poe went to live with his aunt, Maria Clemm, and her daughter Virginia in Baltimore. Poe found his creative spirit revived here and began writing again in earnest, composing a number of short stories and winning a literary contest with his story, "MS Found in a Bottle." His work attracted the attention of J.P. Kennedy, who helped Poe become the editor of the *Southern Literary Messenger* in Richmond. With this job, the prodigal son had returned home. But it wouldn't last. Poe found refuge from his depression, and found it often, in alcohol. While his work was exemplary and insightful, drinking cost Poe his job.

In 1836, Poe married his cousin Virginia Clemm, who was 13 years old. With his child-bride in tow, Poe headed north once again in 1837, this time to New York City, bolstered by both his wife and his hopes of owning his own literary publication. Poe failed in creating his own magazine but found work in Philadelphia editing *Burton's Gentleman's Magazine* and *Graham's Magazine*. By 1844, Poe was confident enough to try his hand again in New York City and found success there working for the *Evening Mirror* and the *Broadway Journal*. *The Raven and Other Poems* came out a year later, a volume of poetry that announced the arrival of a bold writing voice with the force and power of a clarion call. But while Poe was meeting with success in his work, his private life continued to be tinged by loss and tragedy.

In 1847, Poe's wife died. She was 24 at the time, the same age his mother had been when she died. Poe, already disturbed by death and the macabre, was devastated by the loss of his wife. Only 38, but victimized by the death of two beloved women in his life, Poe examined his own mortality. He began wandering late into the night. Worried friends often found the distressed writer at Virginia's grave, weeping and wailing. Virginia's death spurred him to return to Richmond briefly in 1848 and again in 1849. In Richmond, Poe revived his relationship with his forbidden childhood sweetheart, the former Elmira Royster. She had married a Mr. Shelton, but, like Poe, had lost her spouse unexpectedly. Poe reached out from the darkness of his soul and found the hand of Elmira ready and willing to lead him into the light. For once, Poe was able to give up drugs and alcohol. The two found an affinity, leading to a time Poe would call "the happiest he had known for years." He spoke optimistically about the future, flush with love for Elmira and basking in the glow of his spreading fame and acclaim.

In September 1849, Poe gave a reading at the Exchange Hotel, with 300 guests each paying $5 to hear the writer himself present works such as "The Raven." The $1500 he received would be the most money he ever had in his possession at one time. On September 25, Poe made his way to Talavera at 2315 West Grace Street, home of the Tally family. By all accounts, he passed the evening in high spirits and was even coaxed into reading "The Raven" once again. No one could have known it would be the last reading Poe would ever give.

The frontispiece of a 1903 edition of The Works of Edgar Allan Poe *shows a scene from* "The Raven."

Despite his earlier optimism, when Poe left Talavera his mood had changed markedly. Legend states that as Poe turned to bid farewell to his hosts, he lifted his hat. At that exact moment, a meteor arced its way across the sky directly over his head and vanished in the east. Poe saw the celestial object as an omen.

Due to leave for the north once again in order to bring his former mother-in-law and aunt, Maria Clemm, south for his wedding to Elmira, Poe told his fiancée before leaving that he felt that he would never see her again. Poe was supposed to be away for only two weeks, but his fears proved to be grounded. He would never again return to Richmond; less than two weeks later, Edgar Allan Poe would be dead.

The circumstances surrounding his death are mysterious, clouded by speculation. What is known is that Poe left Richmond without any luggage. His bags were packed and left behind at his residence, the Swan Tavern. In the early hours of the morning before his train to Baltimore, he woke a local shopkeeper to have a pair of boots repaired. He then boarded his train and was gone. Those who saw him would later recall that all seemed fine, that while Poe appeared in good spirits, he was decidedly not drunk on them. In Baltimore, Poe was invited to a party. There, he was offered a drink, his hosts apparently unaware that Poe had struggled for years with alcohol abuse and that he had managed to become sober. Why Poe accepted the drink isn't exactly clear; some, like Virginia ghost writer L.B. Taylor, Jr., speculate that he didn't want to risk offending his gracious hosts. The drink ignited something deep within the heart of Poe, his resolve not to drink giving way.

Poe vanished for five days, resurfacing in a Baltimore bar-room, where he was found unconscious in an armchair. Some suspect that Poe had a complete relapse and tumbled fully and completely into alcohol, allowing himself every indulgence on a five-day bender. He was dirty, his clothes tattered, his face unkempt. The $1500 he had earned from speaking at the Exchange Hotel was gone. He was rushed to hospital where doctors determined that he was suffering from extreme dehydration. The membranes in his brain were swollen and inflamed, a condition the doctors diagnosed as a violent brain fever. By this point, there was little that could be done. Edgar Allan Poe died on October 7, 1849. Yet, even in death, Poe would not find the quiet he seemed to crave so desperately.

A cousin commissioned a headstone for Poe's grave, but on the day that it was to be erected in Westminster Cemetery in Baltimore, an accident involving a freight train resulted in the destruction of the tombstone. Instead, Poe's final resting place was marked with a sandstone lot marker inscribed with the number 80. Or was it his final resting place? It seemed that both the marker and the body were not buried where they should have been, not placed in their proper plots until 1875.

Surrounded in death as he was by the ineptness of the living, Poe was unable to find eternal rest. It's said that he haunts Talavera, the last standing home in Richmond he is believed to have visited. In 1975, a group bought the home with plans to renovate it. Residents who have lived within its halls claim the building is haunted. L.B. Taylor, Jr., reports that one former resident was painting his apartment when he heard footsteps in the front foyer. When he went to greet his unexpected visitor, he discovered that he was alone. Another answered the door for two friends and could not have been more surprised when one of them remarked that there was a ghost standing behind him. The specter was described as that of a friendly man, with dark eyes and dark hair. Still another believed that something would climb into bed with him, that while he couldn't see who or what it was, the pillow next to him would clearly depress beneath the head of the spirit. Then there are the usual reports of cold spots throughout the home, of dogs loathing the home.

If it is indeed the spirit of Poe who continues to walk the storied halls of Talavera, then one can only hope that he has found happiness. After all, he has returned to Richmond, the one place where he was able to escape, if for just a brief time, the ghosts of his past.

PENNSYLVANIA
Mad Anthony Wayne

This story is a selection from Dan Asfar's Ghost Stories of Pennsylvania.

He is one of Pennsylvania's favorite sons: General Anthony Wayne, the 18th-century Revolutionary War hero who gave over 20 of his 51 years in staunch service to the United States. He was both a fearless soldier whose heart thrilled in the chaos of battle and a careful general who never made command decisions without proper deliberation. But above all, Wayne was gifted with an amazing knack at pulling off major victories when the people of the fledgling United States most needed them. And while countless individuals threw their lives into building the young country, few could boast such stunning success at repelling America's enemies as could the Pennsylvania-born general.

The name Anthony Wayne probably doesn't figure largely in the lives of most Pennsylvanians today, but the general's legacy is apparent on any map of the state. In addition to the municipalities of Wayne, Waynesboro and Waynesburg, nine townships and one county bear his name. For those who choose not to believe in an afterlife, such widespread posthumous recognition may be considered as close to immortality as an individual can get.

According to the following tale, however, a person can achieve an entirely different sort of immortality, regardless of place names and legendary acclaim. In addition to his name, one might say that Wayne's very remains are spread across the state. Some of the general is respectfully buried in the state's northwest corner, in Presque Isle, while other parts are quietly resting in the southwest corner, in the small hamlet of

Radnor in Chester County. The rest of him is scattered any-where between. Such a bizarre state of postmortem affairs—in addition to an untimely death at the peak of his career—might impel the spirit of Anthony Wayne to haunt the state that bred him.

Wayne was born in Radnor on January 1, 1745; not much about his early life indicated that he would achieve the status of a living legend. The only thing that really stood out about young Wayne was his fervent love for all matters military. A mediocre student, he owed most of his opportunities to the favors of patronage and his family's lofty social standing. After a failed attempt at land surveying while he was in his early 20s, he returned to Radnor to work with his father, helping on the family farm and tannery. At the time, enthusi-asm and influence were enough to make one an officer in the Continental Army. On January 3, 1776, Wayne was commis-sioned as colonel of the Fourth Pennsylvania Battalion—it would prove the start of long and illustrious military career.

He distinguished himself as one of the revolution's pre-eminent military figures, capable of molding any group of men into a premier fighting force. Although cautious with his strategies, the dauntless general was not reluctant to join the front lines and roar in the face of the enemy. This ten-dency to revel in the physical dangers of battle earned him the sobriquet "Mad" Anthony Wayne, one of the more illus-trious names to go down in the annals of American history.

The first battalion Wayne commanded covered the retreat of the American army out of Canada after the battle of Three Rivers. Promoted to brigadier general following his command of Fort Ticonderoga, Wayne fought next at Brandywine Creek, where he held back the British army while Washington and his defeated force retreated to safety. Remaining in the thick of the action throughout the rest of the war, Anthony Wayne was already a famous officer when he won his illustrious victory at Stony Point. The legendary attack took place on July 16, 1779. That evening, Mad Anthony personally led a bayonet attack on the British fort. The general was grazed by a musket during the approach and had to be carried over the parapet by his men, but he remained in command of his unit until the battle was over, bellowing orders over the clash of combat as the American soldiers captured the fort's flag and took over 500 British prisoners. Stony Point was a major morale boost for the revolution, which had won too few military victories against the British Army. After the colonies won their independence, the war hero returned to civilian life.

But just as it was before the war, Wayne was less successful in civilian life than he was in the military. Indeed, after a failed attempt at running a plantation in Georgia and a number of botched political ambitions, Mad Anthony considered himself lucky that sufficient unrest on the continent still required a man of his abilities. Hostile Indians and a persistent British presence west of the Ohio River impelled George Washington to create a standing American army. Anthony Wayne was chosen as the commander-in-chief of the country's first army.

On August 20, 1794, Wayne led the Legion of the United States to a resounding victory at the Battle of Fallen Timbers, defeating the war chief Little Turtle and the Miami Confederacy that had assembled under him. Like a victorious Caesar returning from Gaul, Mad Anthony Wayne was at the peak of his career when he rode back into Pennsylvania in the winter of 1796. Some historians claim that his popularity was such that even the title of president was within his reach. Of this, we can never be certain. On his way back to Pittsburgh, he became ill with gout. He would never beat the illness. Whatever ambitions he entertained died with him along the shores of Lake Erie. He passed away in the recently constructed blockhouse and was given a soldier's burial under the flagpole. So passed away one of America's greatest.

But his story does not end there. Thirteen years later, Wayne's son, Isaac, made the trip from Chester County to Erie with the intent of taking his father's remains back to the family plot in Radnor. Everyone involved in exhuming the general's corpse must have been shocked to discover that his body was remarkably well preserved. Isaac was understandably unwilling to transport the rotting corpse of his father across the state in the back of his wagon. Instead, he consulted a doctor who recommended that the remains be boiled in a caldron, thus separating the dead general's bones from his tissue.

Isaac followed the doctor's advice. The fleshy remains of Mad Anthony Wayne that were left in the bottom of the pot were once again buried in Erie. The general's bones, unfortunately, had no such luck. Legend has it that a good number them were jolted from the wagon on the way back. As Isaac made his way down what is now U.S. Route 322, the wagon lifted and swung over the rocky, heavily rutted road, leaving a rough trail of the general's bones from Erie to Radnor. After a ceremonial burial in St. David's Church in Radnor on July 4, 1809, what was left of Wayne's skeleton was buried in the family plot.

But according to countless eyewitnesses, his rest has not been peaceful. In fact, on every New Year's Day since he was buried, an apparition of the dead general has been spotted along Route 322, mounted on a phantom horse. The figure tears down the highway at an incredible speed, passing straight through anything in his way without breaking his stride. Some eyewitnesses have been able to make out the details of his uniform—the epaulets on his shoulders, his saber bouncing on his side and his tricorne hat sitting atop his powdered wig.

The same people have also reported that his blank eyes glance from one side of the road to the other, almost as if to search for something that is lying on the side of the highway. Such accounts give credence to the popular theory that Mad Anthony's ghost is looking for the bones that were not buried with him in Radnor. In this scenario, the apparition shows Wayne's supernatural discontent at having his remains disturbed and strewn across the state.

There are other theories as well. A few of his biographers write about how difficult it must have been for the head-strong general to face such a meek end so soon after winning glory on the battlefield. If Mad Anthony Wayne had his choice, he would have surely preferred to fall in a hail of musket fire than in the quiet comfort of the Erie blockhouse. His last breaths must have brought with them the realization that if his frail mortal frame had not failed him, his victory at Fallen Timbers may have cast him into the highest echelons of society, perhaps even as far as the White House. The world was finally his oyster, but he could not even get out of bed. Those who shudder at the thought of such frustrated ambition are more inclined to believe that Mad Anthony's apparition has more to do with the general's anger at never being able to enjoy the fruits of his labors.

Either way, drivers on U.S. Route 322 on New Year's Day should beware. Unless motorists don't mind having a 200-year-old ghost pass straight through their car, it would be wise for them to give any ghostly horseman in the rearview mirror the right of way.

WISCONSIN
The Return of La Salle

Robert Cavalier, the Sieur de la Salle, was born in Rouen in 1643 and came to North America to explore the Great Lakes region. He hoped to discover a passage to China and the South Sea. He never did find the fabled passage, but he did find something else: an opportunity to make a profit.

La Salle put aside his intentions of becoming a Jesuit priest to pursue dreams of wealth in the fur trade. He established a residence on the St. Lawrence at Lachine, explored the wilderness and began learning the customs and languages of the American Indian tribes the fur trade relied on. By 1669, he began moving westward to collect furs from Indian tribes such as the Huron and the Mackinac, who made their homes along the shores of the Great Lakes.

La Salle had a 60-foot ship built and christened it the *Griffin*, and it came to be the first sailing vessel to appear on the Great Lakes. It set sail in 1679 from the mouth of Cayuga Creek and after a month, during which time it soldiered through heavy storms on Lake Huron, the *Griffin* arrived at Pointe St. Ignace. From there, the ship proceeded to Green Bay and docked at Washington Island, where La Salle's men had acquired a large number of furs from the Mackinaws. It's said that when these Indians first laid eyes upon the *Griffin*, they called it a floating fortress. The Iroquois, in fear, considered the ship a threat to the Great Spirit and placed a curse on the ship.

Grand as she was, the *Griffin* was destined never to make another journey. Having loaded the ship with furs, La Salle sent his crew and ship away while he set off in a canoe to explore the St. Joseph River and find a link to the mighty

Sieur de la Salle, an early explorer of the Great Lakes

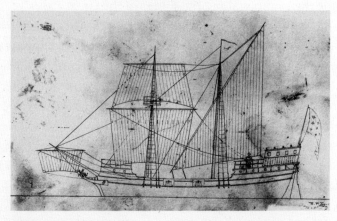

An early drawing of the Griffin, *now a ghost ship seen in Green Bay Harbor*

Mississippi. As for the *Griffin*, it set sail for Niagara, a destination it would never reach. The *Griffin* just vanished. Did the Iroquois curse condemn the ship? Or were there less mystical reasons for its disappearance?

Some believe that the ship was overcome by fierce storms along the lake, while others theorize that it was attacked and burned by Indians as it passed through the Straits of Mackinaw. One of the more enduring hypotheses suggests that La Salle's own crew had destroyed the *Griffin*. Fed up with their captain, the crew took advantage of La Salle's absence to plunder the rich cargo of furs and then scuttle the ship. The *Griffin*'s fate remains a mystery. Although divers have searched for its remains for centuries, the remains have never been found. Many have claimed to have seen the wreckage in places such as a cove near Tobermory, Ontario, but definitive proof remains out of reach.

Still others along Green Bay Harbor insist that the *Griffin* sails the Great Lakes to this day. Those living in this lakeside community are particularly vigilant on foggy nights. They watch expectantly, hoping to catch a glimpse of the *Griffin*'s ghostly form as it cuts through the waters.

As for La Salle, the *Griffin*'s loss did not hamper the great explorer. With his faithful friend, ship-builder Henri de Tonti, La Salle explored the Mississippi River to its mouth in the Gulf of Mexico. He claimed the entire basin for France, naming the area Louisiana in honor of the French king, Louis XIV. He met his end shortly after. Charged with establishing a fort in the crown's new possession, La Salle lost his way and landed at Matagorda Bay, Texas. Mutineers killed La Salle. His crew had lost patience with their captain while he blundered helplessly along the coast, unable to find the mouth of the Mississippi. Despite his woeful and pathetic end, La Salle's contributions to the early European exploration of this continent cannot be understated. His legacy lives on in both the state of Louisiana and in Green Bay Harbor, where the *Griffin* continues to sail its waters, a ghostly ship destined never to reach its port.

North Carolina
Blackbeard's Ghost

Today, Ocracoke Island is part of the barrier islands forming the Outer Banks of North Carolina as well as the Cape Hatteras National Seashore. With the Atlantic on one side and Pamlico Sound on the other, it is accessible only by water or air. Boasting 16 miles of shoreline and beach, the village of Ocracoke lies on the southern end of the island and has been on the National Register of Historic Places since 1990. It's a quaint little place, where speed limits rarely exceed 24 mph and where streets can be clogged during the high season with sunburned visitors eager to explore all the resources Ocracoke has to offer. There is the fishing, the surfing, the camping, the swimming and the tanning.

For those who'd prefer to enjoy themselves away from the beach and the surf, there is the history, a past brought to life by the 1823 Ocracoke Lighthouse, one of the oldest on the Atlantic coast; the Banker Ponies, descendants of horses first brought to the Outer Banks by Sir Walter Raleigh; and the British Cemetery, interred with the bodies of four British seamen who washed ashore, casualties of a German submarine attack upon their ship. The inlet at Ocracoke was inhabited centuries before the first European explorers came to its shores and before painter John White immortalized the Outer Banks in 1585. Little has changed at Ocracoke as time has passed. People were attracted by its isolated locale and rugged beauty then and they still are today, but while people come today seeking recreation and relaxation, those in the past came to Ocracoke to hide and escape. The waters of Ocracoke, after all, are known to be the final resting place of one of the more famous pirates, Edward Teach, better known as Blackbeard.

Little is known about the early years of Teach's life, but it is believed that he was born in Bristol, England, in 1680. From there, he embarked upon a life of piracy during Queen Anne's War in the early 18th century. Historians note that while pirates are often portrayed as fearsome renegades, they were once invaluable in the struggle for seafaring supremacy, employed by competing countries, such as England and Spain, to harass rival commercial ships that might enhance the wealth and standing of another nation. The British Empire was known to hire pirates to raid other ships so that the Crown might add to its wealth; these pirates were known as privateers, required to pay a fifth of their profits to the Crown. For many, piracy was the means to amass wealth quickly, a way to move up through social ranks predicated upon having vast sums of money. Pirates could work for a few years and then retire to a quiet, anonymous life of affluence and influence in England. For the population at large, pirates provided goods at rates lower than what might be found going through the proper channels. Regardless, pirates were still a lawless element, and when wars were fought and finished, a class of tough seamen had been created, not all of whom were willing to go gently and quietly into a new way of life. They continued to raid the seas, doing what came easiest to them. It wasn't long before those who had fed their existence found that they had to police an element that had once been one of their greater assets.

This was the lifestyle a young Edward Teach stepped into early in the 18th century when he served aboard privateer ships sailing from Jamaica during Queen Anne's War. At the conclusion of the war, Teach did what a large number of privateers did—he joined the fraternity of the Brethren of the Coast and became a pirate. He headed to New Providence in the Bahamas, a location largely controlled by pirates. There,

Teach came to the attention of Captain Benjamin Hornigold, reportedly one of the fiercest and most capable pirates then operating from New Providence. Hornigold was impressed by Teach, the way the young man thrived under pressure and excelled at combat; Teach was a natural, blessed with ability and skill. Before long, Hornigold had given Teach his own command, that of a ship seized in a fierce skirmish in 1716.

In 1717, Teach captured the *Concord*, a large Dutch-built French guineaman. He redesigned the ship according to his specifications and renamed the ship the *Queen Anne's Revenge.* The two would later become synonymous with terror, the mere mention of either man or vessel enough to incite fear in the heart of even the ablest of men. It seems that even then individuals were aware of the power of an image. Teach was not nearly as fearsome or terrifying as many believed him to be.

Teach was aware of his reputation and cultivated an image to play up the more ridiculous elements of his legend. He grew a beard to an extraordinary length. Coarse and braided, the beard was dark as pitch, twisted into tiny braids held in place by a variety of ribbons. The whole arrangement covered Teach's face, the perfect complement to his thick eyebrows. With an imposing and impressive build, Teach cut a fearsome figure indeed. In battle, Teach was fond of tucking lit fuse cords under the brim of his hat. The cords, treated with saltpeter and lime water, burned slowly, the wisps of smoke curling lazily around his head. Occasionally, Teach would stoop down to his cannons, igniting the powder in them with his fuses. It may have been a little unorthodox, but his appearance did have an impact. Few had the will to resist Blackbeard when confronted with both his look and legend.

Blackbeard the pirate still searches for his head near Ocracoke Island.

Despite everything, Blackbeard was not a killer. If his victims submitted willingly, all they stood to lose was their property. Of course, if Blackbeard met with resistance, he could be cruel and vicious. In one cited example, a hapless victim refused to give Blackbeard a ring. Blackbeard, refusing to be denied, took both the ring and the finger wearing it. He is also believed to have shot one of his own men to remind his crew of who their captain was. Blackbeard could be at once merciful and merciless. Captains of ships Blackbeard had plundered often exaggerated elements of the latter, with hopes of saving their now questionable reputations.

Blackbeard sailed through the West Indies and the Atlantic Coast of North America. While there, Blackbeard found the Ocracoke Inlet in North Carolina's Outer Banks. The site appealed to him; numerous shoals and inlets in the area aided concealment, and if he was ever to be discovered, his knowledge of the topography would allow him to elude his enemies easily. And, from the Ocracoke Inlet, Blackbeard could observe merchant ships coming and going and wait patiently for the attack. Merchant ships were often caught unaware. No wonder then that this isolated barrier island became a favorite haunt of Blackbeard's. When he surrendered in 1717 to take advantage of the King's pardon of all pirate crimes in that year, the pirate formerly known as Edward Teach retired to life with his 14th wife in Bath, North Carolina, just across Pamlico Sound from Ocracoke. By this time, Blackbeard had plundered an estimated 25 ships and accrued a large fortune. But he couldn't resist himself for long. Quiet retirement didn't suit his temperament.

Within six months, Blackbeard was once again plundering the Atlantic coast along the Carolinas and Virginia. To ensure minimal interference with his activities, Blackbeard shared a percentage of his gains with North Carolina Governor Charles Eden. For a while, Blackbeard sailed the seas freely, but times were changing. The British colonies were developing rapidly and trade was becoming increasingly important to their continued success. Blackbeard stood in the way of that progress and citizens of the coast were beginning to tire of Blackbeard's constant presence. The people of North Carolina, realizing that their own governor would be ineffectual in bringing an end to pirate activity along the coast, turned to Virginia Governor Alexander Spotswood, who had dedicated himself to routing the scourge known as Blackbeard.

In November 1718, Spotswood sent out an English Navy Lieutenant named Robert Maynard to take care of Blackbeard. Two armed sloops, *Jane* and *The Ranger*, set off for Ocracoke where Blackbeard had anchored his ship, *The Adventure*, with 25 of his men to host a pirates' festival. Realizing what was happening, Blackbeard raised anchor and guided *The Adventure* through a narrow channel with hidden sand bars. The two sloops grounded themselves, but Maynard, commanding from *The Ranger*, ordered men on both boats to throw their water barrels overboard. The sloops were freed and they continued their pursuit. Within short order, cannon fire tore through the air and Pamlico Sound was transformed into a battleground.

The Adventure had superior firepower and *The Ranger* bore the full brunt of her attack. Maynard quickly saw that there was little he could hope to do against Blackbeard from his vessel; he would have to draw Blackbeard onto his ship where the cannons of *The Adventure* would no longer be an advantage. He ordered his men below deck. Blackbeard, seeing a deserted ship, presumed that the ship was now helpless. His assumption was a prelude to weakness.

Blackbeard and his men boarded the ship, where Maynard and his crew engaged the intruders in fierce combat. Maynard and Blackbeard stood toe to toe, each one pulling a pistol and firing. When they were too close for pistols, the two drew their swords. The situation looked grim for Maynard when his blade broke under the force of a Blackbeard stroke. But just as Blackbeard prepared to run Maynard through, a Royal Marine, coming to the aid of his fallen captain, stabbed Blackbeard in the neck with his saber.

Yet, Blackbeard did not fall; only after being hacked, slashed and shot repeatedly did the pirate finally succumb. He had been shot 5 times and stabbed over 20 times before he fell to the deck of Maynard's ship. It is said that before he died, he told his 13th wife that he would return and that his arrival would be heralded by the sound of cannon fire.

Maynard severed Blackbeard's head and hung it from his bowsprit as a warning to others. The body was dumped unceremoniously into the Atlantic. Legend says that the body circled Maynard's ship three times before disappearing beneath the waves.

Today, there are those who live along Pamlico Sound who claim that every now and then, they will hear the sound of cannon fire and see, off in the mists of Ocracoke, Blackbeard's ghost ship sailing over the water. Others have seen his headless ghost wandering about the shore in search of his head, his voice and footsteps echoing through the air. Unexplained lights on the coast are fondly referred to as Teach's Light, the ethereal glow from the lamp that Blackbeard is rumored to carry to help in his search. It's believed that Blackbeard continues his search out of fear that when he enters Hell, the devil will be unable to recognize him without his trademark black beard. So he continues to haunt the land he loved so much in life, forever cursing Robert Maynard for consigning him to this fate.

6
Cemeteries

Georgia
Oakland Cemetery

While the dead may be buried, their spirits live on in the hearts and memories of those who knew them during their time on this earth. Indeed, while a cemetery is primarily a home for the dead, it is also a place where the past has taken root and flourished. To walk a cemetery is to walk with history. In Atlanta, the past and present converge in the Oakland Cemetery. Citizens from all walks of life are interred there—those prominent and those not so prominent—all contributing their voice to the chorus of Atlanta's history. And particularly at certain times of the year, this voice becomes much more literal than metaphorical, and the cries of the dead are audible to the living.

The history of the Oakland Cemetery is fascinating in its own right, even if there were no phantom whispers heard there. In 1821, farmers began to arrive to the area that became Atlanta, attracted by the offer of land lotteries. More people arrived when the site became the terminus of the Georgia Railroad and the Western and Atlantic Railroad, creating by 1837 a rough and tumble area of rail hands and prostitutes. By 1847, this town of 10,000 voted to change its name from Marthasville to Atlanta. Young people were drawn to the town and its thriving economy. But as the population grew, so too did the need for public burial grounds. Three years later, the self-proclaimed founding fathers of Atlanta purchased six acres on the east part of town for use as a cemetery. The first man to be buried at the cemetery was a Chicago doctor who passed away in 1850 while in Atlanta for a convention. Terrified as he was of being buried alive, Dr. James Nissen had asked for his throat to be slit before he was lowered into the ground. It was. After 17 years, the cemetery spanned 88 acres. In 1872, what had been City Cemetery became Oakland Cemetery, so named because of the numerous oak trees on the property. By the late 19th century, the final plots of Oakland Cemetery were sold. Buried within the original six acres of land are the early influential of Atlanta, including 6 state governors, 24 mayors, senators and representatives. Dr. Joe Jacobs is buried here; he owned a pharmacist where one day an entrepreneur created a concoction he called Coca-Cola. Bob Jones, winner of the Grand Slam of golf in the 1920s, lies in the same ground as Margaret Mitchell, author of *Gone With the Wind*. Those less famous are here too, buried in Potter's Field; there are over 17,000, each unidentified but remembered nonetheless.

Today, little has changed in Oakland Cemetery, besides the paving and bricking over of the old dirt roads. With its elaborate headstones, sculptures and mausoleums, it is considered a Victorian-era cemetery. But there are other ages to see here too.

A plot of land called the Black Section is where, before the Civil War, black slaves were buried, identified by both their names and their owners'. After the war, blacks continued to be buried here. And, just west of the original six acres stands a 65-foot obelisk made of granite from Stone Mountain. When first erected, it was the tallest structure in Atlanta. This monument marks off the Confederate section; interred within are the bodies of unknown Confederate and Union soldiers. Notables lying here include Alexander Hamilton and Brigadier General W.S. Stephen.

In July 1864, Atlanta was home to more than 20,000 people. Shortly after, Sherman began his march through Georgia. By November, fewer than 1000 residents were still in Atlanta when the city began to burn. Bodies of the dead soldiers were piled in trenches in Oakland Cemetery and then buried during the last hours of the attack on Atlanta. Still others arrived from a makeshift hospital blocks away in Cabbagetown. By the end, Oakland Cemetery was the final resting place for over 3000 Confederate and 16 Union soldiers.

Watching over these buried soldiers is the "Lion of Atlanta," a 30,000-pound marble lion, lying on a base 17 feet high. Carved in the likeness of the Lion of Lucerne in Switzerland, the lion lies prostrate, its heart pierced by an arrow, its head cradled by the stars and bars of the Confederate flag, honoring those who died for their ideals. It is here where the past can truly be said to come alive.

In a book entitled *Georgia Ghosts*, Nancy Roberts recounted the experience of a visitor to the cemetery. While standing by the "Lion of Atlanta," the visitor was shocked to hear phantom sounds. Amid rustling leaves, he heard the sounds of weapons clanging. Then, most surprising, voices seemed to be calling from beyond the graves. A roll call of soldiers was heard, as if they were no longer content to be nameless. The same visitor also saw ghostly apparitions moving amid the trees, shadows of fighting soldiers.

Visitors to the cemetery are likely to hear the phantom voices particularly in November or December—likely because it was at that time of the year in 1864 when so many Confederate soldiers were buried. Names are called out and then, against the whispering wind, a number of voices answer in reply. One will hear these voices and know that it is the dead who are speaking, know that what is being heard is the roll call of these soldiers, unknown no longer.

MAINE
The Witch's Foot

As with most significant historical figures, there is a fair bit of controversy surrounding Colonel Jonathan Buck. Intrepid Massachusetts explorer, Revolutionary War hero and founder of the town of Bucksport on the Penobscot River, Buck belongs to that same echelon of Americans as John Smith, Wyatt Earp and Huey Long—men whose courage and natural abilities turned the trials of their times into opportunities for greatness. That being said, Colonel Buck's fame today does not rest so much on the merits of his historical accomplishments but rather on a morbid legend that involves a public burning, a witch's dying curse and an unsettling mark on the deceased colonel's tombstone that is impossible to remove.

There are varying opinions on Jonathan Buck. Some accounts have him being a cold-hearted womanizer; others have written him as an ambitious opportunist, intent on carving out a personal empire. And then there are those biographers who have cast him as a religious puritan, incapable of any feeling besides a profound love for scripture.

Buck's personality might be shrouded in mystery, but the solid historical facts of his life are impressive enough to write a narrative of their own. He was one of the leading men in a 1762 expedition from Massachusetts to the Penobscot River in what is now Maine. It was their mission to set up six townships in the countryside along the Penobscot. One of these settlements, Bucksport, would be named after Jonathan Buck, who had commandeered the *Sally*, the vessel that transported the 352 pioneers into the unsettled territory. Spending the next decade sweating through the backbreaking labor of making homes from the wild landscape, the colonel put his money and muscle into the plantation that would eventually bare his namesake.

But the pioneers' labors were interrupted by the outbreak of the Revolutionary War. A British fleet anchored in the Penobscot Bay cut Buck and the other settlers off from Massachusetts, arresting the arrival of any supplies into the struggling little colony. Thrown into the vortex of armed conflict, Buck spent the next several years at war with Imperial Britain. He was present at the siege of Fort George in 1779, where the Patriots suffered one of the worst naval defeats in American history. The next day, he and his family vacated the fledgling township. Jonathan Buck, along with his wife and daughter, made the 200-mile walk from the Penobscot to Haverhill, Massachusetts, leaving the home-stead they put 10 years of their lives into behind to be razed by the British. Buck was 65 years old when the War of Independence was over, but age did not stop the tenacious colonel from returning to Maine. He managed the recon-struction of the town, rebuilding everything the British had destroyed in 1779. Recognizing the role Buck and his sons played in the formation of their town, the settlers honored the patriarch in 1792 by naming the plantation Bucksport, after the colonel who had built it from the ground up twice. Jonathan lived in the town that bore his name for nearly three years, before death claimed him in March 1795.

These are the landmark events of Jonathan Buck's life, the historical events that made the colonel into one of Maine's first men. But it is one historical footnote in Jonathan's life that has cast the Bucksport founder into the canon of super-natural folklore. For it isn't the colonel's achievements that have made his tombstone the most visited gravesite in Bucksport Cemetery. There aren't many people who argue over the political, military or commercial significance of Buck's actions in the 18th century. It is the mark of the witch's foot on his tombstone that has kept Jonathan alive as a topic of conversation. And the different explanations for the mysterious mark have been responsible for the liveliest speculations regarding what kind of man Jonathan Buck was.

The most popular version of the Bucksport legend has Jonathan Buck, a Puritan Justice of the Peace, presiding over a trial where a local woman is accused of witchcraft. Buck found the woman guilty as charged and sentenced her to death by burning. On the day of her death, the woman added to the spectacle of her execution by issuing a baleful curse at Jonathan Buck. "The only comfort I draw from my death, colonel, is that you will follow me shortly," the old woman screamed at the man who had condemned her to a fiery demise. "You will soon die, and when you do, I will put my mark on your tombstone. My feet will appear under your accursed name, a reminder to all who follow that Jonathan Buck condemned a woman to burning."

It was said that after the execution, the colonel became a fitful sleeper, muttering through dreams every night. He died, just as the witch foretold, shortly after the fateful execution and was laid to rest under the most impressive monument in Bucksport Cemetery.

It appeared the day after the funeral—a crimson image of a lower leg and foot hanging beneath Buck's name. The Buck family immediately had the eerie blemish sanded from the stone, but it appeared again the next day. The image was cleaned again, only to reappear. This pattern continued throughout the 19th century, with the tombstone being cleaned countless times to no avail. Jonathan's exasperated progeny finally tried replacing the cursed tombstone with another grave marker in the mid-1800s. The next day, everyone was shocked to see the shape of the witch's foot on the new monument, again hanging just under the family name.

Variations of this story cast Jonathan in a more sinister light. This version has Colonel Buck falling for Ida, a beautiful young woman who had recently arrived in town. He took her as his mistress, and things went well for a short while. But after the embers of their illicit affair cooled, Jonathan began scheming on ways to get rid of her. The calculating man didn't want to deal with the potential scandal his ex-lover might cause, so in an act of unmitigated barbarity, he had a crony accuse her of witchcraft. He found her guilty and sentenced her to death.

Tied to the stake, Ida was said to be hysterically afraid, weeping uncontrollably as the pier was lit under her. Then her eyes fell on Jonathan Buck, who was sitting smugly among the townsfolk that had gathered to watch the innocent woman die. She grew livid. "What do you think you have won, Jonathan?" Ida screamed through tears of rage. "I promise you, I'll be dancing on your grave while you burn in the eternal fires of hell."

Jonathan was dead shortly after, and the shape of one of Ida's lower legs and feet appeared on his tombstone. The family did everything it could to remove the blemish, but it kept coming back, located in the exact same place on the monument, where it remains to this very day—just underneath Jonathan's last name.

There are other tales, though none are as widely accepted as the above. Some have even tried to explain the outline of the foot rationally, saying that an impurity in the granite may have changed color as it oxidized over time, forming the legendary impression on the Buck tombstone. But the fact that this same impression would appear on the same place on two different tombstones seems too much of a coincidence, and most have disregarded this theory.

While we might never know what kind of man Jonathan Buck was, the mysterious foot on his gravestone and the legends that go along with it suggest a dark side to the man's life. Whether he was an egocentric killer or a magistrate trying to do his job, one thing does seem certain—someone from the past seems intent on saying something about the man, and given the nature of the message, it cannot be good.

IDAHO
Boot Hill Cemetery

Idaho City is a community of just over 300 people. It is the seat of Boise County and a place where the past looms large over everything. Buildings erected in the 1860s stand still, among them the *Idaho World* newspaper offices, the old schoolhouse and courthouse, testifying silently to Idaho City's boom and bust during the gold rush. And up above what is now an airstrip is Boot Hill Cemetery. Still visible on the tombstones are the names of the miners who sought wealth, the men who crossed them and the women who loved them. The saplings are now giant trees; the tombstones they once complemented they now threaten to overwhelm. The wooden fences sag. But still, the dead walk the land. In Idaho City, the miners and prospectors still seek their fortunes, even from beyond the grave.

In the years leading up to the founding of Idaho City, the Union was in peril; states were engaged in war, each fighting to maintain their beliefs and preserve what they perceived to be the spirit and intent of the American Constitution. The conflict threatened to consign to history everything such

Boot Hill Cemetery is likely haunted by the ghosts of gold miners from Idaho City.

American revolutionaries as Washington and Jefferson had fought for: the existence of a great democratic republic.

But while warfare gripped the attentions of the states, the concerns of those settlers exploring the western reaches of the continent were far more local. They were motivated not by any particular ideology but by that dark compulsion beating within the hearts of all: the compulsion to acquire wealth. They explored the opportunities to acquire fortunes in the silver and gold mines throughout the newly formed territories. Avarice both sustained and suffocated these prospectors. It is an idea rendered in the solemnity and awful beauty of the Boot Hill Cemetery in Idaho City, a site where just 23 of the first 200 buried here were laid to rest because of natural causes.

In 1860, 10 prospectors, led by Captain E.D. Pierce, entered the Nez Perce Reservation. In a month they found what they were looking for. Wilbur Bassett, panning along Canal Gulch, discovered gold. When word of the discovery reached an expectant audience, the news ignited a rush of migration to the area that would eventually become known as Idaho, the Gem State.

Just half a year after Bassett's discovery along Canal Gulch, 1600 claims had been staked. Towns with names like Lewiston and Pierce City were sprouting all through the area, connected first by paths that would accommodate only pack-horses and mules. As they grew, the paths became roads, and stagecoaches, once a rare sight along the horizon, became commonplace. Prospectors came from Sacramento, San Francisco and Vancouver, lured by the promise of gold as abundant as the blades of prairie grass. Those who found areas too crowded for their liking set off for less-populated regions. Before long, the Florence Basin, where the gold was discovered, was overrun with miners and said to have produced over $600,000 worth of gold, adjusted for inflation, a day. But even that amount wasn't enough to satisfy voracious appetites; it only whetted them.

Twelve men, led by H.D. Fogus, discovered gold in the Boise Basin in 1862, and when people heard that there might be more gold there than in the Florence, the Boise Basin was soon teeming with men and women eager to seek their fortunes. Placerville, Centerville and Bannock City...these towns developed overnight. The rapid and mass influx of people to the area led to the creation of the Idaho Territory, with Lewiston established as its capital. But while Lewiston may have been the seat of power, everyone knew that the action was in what was once Bannock City, but what is now immortalized as Idaho City. Less than a year after Fogus' gold discovery, thousands had swarmed into the Boise Basin, with over 6000 migrating to Idaho City.

Within three years, 10,000 people called Idaho City home, and those seeking to profit off of the miners' presence arrived en masse. At its height, Idaho City had more than 250 businesses lining its wooden boulevards. It boasted an opera and theater house, tailors, breweries, pool halls, drug stores and headquarters for the *Idaho World Paper*. The oldest Masonic Hall west of the Mississippi was there, and, most profitable of all, the saloon and brothel. With so many people concentrated in such a small area, each trying to get their respective hands on a share of the rumored wealth of the Boise Basin, life in Idaho City was not for the faint-hearted. Over 23 law offices were kept in a perpetual state of toil as they handled disputes over competing mining claims. Those who preferred not to deal with lawyers took matters into their own hands. Alcohol was cheap in Idaho City; life was cheaper. A hanging or a shooting was never far off.

The dead were taken to what became known as Boot Hill Cemetery. Tombstones were placed inside areas bordered by elaborate wooden fences, often accompanied by a sapling. The tombstones testify to the rough and heady life in the early days of the Gold Rush. But for most, the danger was worth the risk. It's said that in Idaho City's boom, more than $250 million worth of gold was extracted from the Boise Basin.

Gold was the reason for Idaho City's boom, but when the gold ran dry, so did the town. With so much of the valuable ore mined each day, it wasn't long before the boom became a bust. An estimated three million ounces were taken from the mines; it became harder for prospectors to get their hands on the metal and the rewards no longer outweighed the investment. Hordes of people abandoned the Boise Basin. Idaho City, once rollicking and rolling, saw its prosperity fade.

But a walk though Boot Hill Cemetery reveals that for some the heady days of the gold rush never ended. People have reported seeing men walking in and around the tombstones, garbed in the dress of the late-19th-century prospector. Others have heard snatches of conversation in Chinese. These phantom voices are the legacy of the thousands of Chinese who immigrated in the 1860s to work in the laundries, herb houses, restaurants and gravel bars of Idaho. Apparitions of these settlers can also be seen, dressed in traditional Chinese clothing.

These various ghosts of Idaho City appear only to vanish into the air from which they came, now mere shadows of a once booming and bustling community.

ILLINOIS
Resurrection Mary

Down along Archer Avenue in Chicago is the optimistically named Resurrection Cemetery. Here the living have a chance to catch a glimpse of an afterlife, to see resurrection in the form of the beautiful young spirit known as Mary. Her origins are shrouded in mystery; her appearance always raises more questions than answers. The enigma of Mary only adds to her appeal and allure. Who is she? What does she want? How did she die? Why does she prefer to appear to men rather than women? These questions do not have any definite solutions. There are a number of educated guesses though and then, of course, there are the many accounts of Resurrection Mary, as she has been christened, appearing and challenging the rational mind.

Reportedly Mary first appeared in 1936 at the Liberty Grove Hall and Ballroom in southwest Chicago. Jerry Palus, out for the evening, was looking to meet some girls and have some fun. He found himself transfixed by a beautiful blonde with devastatingly blue eyes, shimmering and sparkling like a diamond amid the crowd in her snowy white cocktail dress and white satin dancing shoes. Palus danced with her throughout the night and while he was enjoying himself, he couldn't help wondering why this girl, so radiant and inviting on the dance floor, was in conversation coldly impersonal. When she allowed him a kiss as the ballroom was closing, he was further intrigued when he discovered how cold and clammy her lips were. But her touch couldn't prepare him for what happened next.

He offered the girl a ride home and she accepted. As he approached the gates of Resurrection Cemetery, she asked him to stop and drop her off. A cemetery certainly is an odd place to drop a girl off, but Palus did as asked; he was already quite fond of this girl in white and wanted to have every chance of seeing her again. So she got out and, being a gentleman, Palus waited to make sure she was safe before he left. It became clear shortly thereafter that the girl with whom he had been dancing was special indeed. He watched her approach the gates and then, before his very eyes, walk through its iron bars as if they didn't exist and then vanish like dew in the warm light of the morning sun. Palus never did figure out what or who he drove to the cemetery that night, but he wouldn't be alone in his confusion and bewilderment for long. Soon police departments were fielding numerous calls from motorists passing along Archer Avenue, all reporting that a woman was trying to jump onto the running boards of their cars. And while Resurrection Mary was never seen again in the Liberty Grove Hall and Ballroom, she found other places to have a good time.

Throughout the years, Mary has been seen at a number of dance establishments. After Liberty, she was seen with some regularity at the Oh Henry Ballroom. In the 1970s, it was at Harlow's on South Cicero Avenue where she would appear mysteriously on the dance floor, standing out sharply in her dated dress among the bell-bottoms and polyester suits. Again, she was standoffish, insular and oblivious to everyone around her. The attention of the staff was drawn to her because no bouncers at any of the club's entrances could recall admitting her. In fact, no one ever saw her leave or enter the club.

Who was Resurrection Mary in life? There a number of theories but none stand up under close scrutiny. The only constant in the hypotheses is that Mary was young, that she died tragically because of the failings of a man and that

Resurrection Cemetery is where she is most likely to be found. In the 1970s, a woman in a white dress was seen wandering the grounds of Resurrection Cemetery late at night. When a motorist saw her, the woman began shaking the iron bars of the cemetery's gates. To the motorist, she looked very much like a woman trapped after hours in the cemetery and just desperate to leave. He reported what he'd seen to a police sergeant but when the officer went to investigate, the woman was gone. The only sign that the motorist hadn't been mistaken in his claims was that the iron bars of the gate were pried apart and marred with the impression of two handprints.

If Mary isn't prying open gates, she's being picked up or dropped off near Resurrection. Recently, she has been dancing outside the gates. Some encounters with the spirit are more gruesome and disturbing. Some drivers passing Archer Avenue slam on their brakes, frantically trying to avoid a pedestrian who appears out of nowhere, wearing a white dress. More often than not, they hit the girl, but when they leave their vehicles to check on their victim, they see the bruised and battered body of the girl disappear.

Her association with the cemetery and habit of getting hit by cars suggests to many that she died in a car accident and is, quite possibly, buried in Resurrection Cemetery. Could she have been Mary Bregavy, a young Polish woman who died in a car crash in 1935 on her way home from the Oh Henry Ballroom? It's doubtful, as Bregavy had short dark hair, not the long blonde tresses of Resurrection Mary. Could she then have been the unfortunate girl who stormed out of the Oh Henry Ballroom one night after a fight with her boyfriend, only to step into the path of an oncoming car? Mary's origins may never be known and for some in Chicago, that's just as well.

While there are those who believe in the spirit of Resurrection Mary, more than a few longtime residents of the Chicago suburb of Justice would rather not acknowledge the presence or the existence of their famous resident. One employee of the cemetery claimed that in all his many years working at Resurrection, he never once saw or heard anything out of the ordinary. Many in the suburb have never seen Mary and now resent the attention the story brings to their quiet community; of course, just because Mary has not appeared to them is no reason to deny her existence. In spite of the skepticism, sightings continue, and some reports hint that it is mostly males who are able to see Resurrection Mary, possibly because one figured prominently in her death.

Two women were exploring the Resurrection Cemetery looking for the ghost of Mary. They found nothing and decided to leave. One of the girls drove the other home before returning to her own place. When she returned home, her boyfriend was waiting for her and watched her drive up and park. When she got out of the car, he asked her where her friend had gone—he had definitely seen someone dressed in white sitting next to his girlfriend in the front seat. Strangely enough, his girlfriend hadn't seen a thing. Many young men have seen Mary dancing outside the cemetery gates and were perturbed when they realized they were only ones capable of seeing her.

In the end, Resurrection Mary continues to haunt both Archer Avenue and the imagination. Questions about her identity will probably never be answered. Perhaps she enjoys being a woman of mystery. And while some resent the sort of attention she draws, the owners of Chet's Melody Lounge probably couldn't be happier; their bar is often the first place shaken motorists stop after encountering Resurrection Mary.

7
Haunted
Universities

NORTH DAKOTA
The West Hall Tunnel

Walking didn't seem like such a bad idea at the time. After all, she must have made the short jaunt from West Hall to Wilkerson Dining Hall over a hundred times. The young University of North Dakota student had her dinner there every day; her feet practically knew the way by themselves. So she didn't think much of the blizzard roaring outside on that fateful December night in 1962. Although she couldn't see the building through all the snow and wasn't wearing much in the way of winter clothing, she couldn't have imagined that the short stroll could be fatal.

That was before she stepped outside into the unusually vicious North Dakota snowstorm. She was lost after about a dozen steps outside, disoriented by the wind, cold and low visibility. She tried returning to her residence, but quickly discovered she didn't know the way back.

No one knows why she ventured out that night; the errand she had to run is now forever lost in the chronicle of the dead. Nor does anyone know how long she struggled in the frigid night, how long she suffered the numbing effects of hypothermia. Regardless of what happened, her frozen corpse was found the next morning about 60 feet from West Hall.

Since then, the University of North Dakota took to constructing tunnels to connect the five dormitories, providing a safe, warm passage to Wilkerson Hall. While this addition was welcomed by students living in residence, disturbing stories began emerging from the West Hall tunnel shortly after the system of walkways was completed.

She has been spotted in the West Hall tunnel countless times over the years, appearing before terrified students late on stormy winter nights. She has been described as quite striking, with short black hair and big dark eyes. Some have said that she appears frightened, desperately looking for a way out of the passage before vanishing into nothingness. Others claim that she looks quite calm, standing motionless and looking blankly ahead, staring straight through frightened witnesses for several moments, only to suddenly disappear without a word. Everyone who has seen her agrees on her startling state of disembodiment. For only the top half of the young woman appears; there has never been a trace of anything under her waist. Her transparent apparition floats about three feet above the ground, without the benefit of feet or legs.

Students' reactions to the young woman have varied considerably. Early sightings were usually panicked. The authorities were called frequently, and for a while there was considerable buzz about the resident ghost haunting the West tunnel. Yet over the passing years, she has appeared before students less and less, even as her legend was entrenched as the University of North Dakota's local haunt.

Today, she appears only during especially violent storms, when the sky swirls with thick white snow and the wind is so strong that houses rattle under the freezing blasts. It is then that the apparition of the hapless young student appears in the safety of the West tunnel, looking beyond bewildered students with mortal fear or utter calm. She floats there for several minutes before fading into the very nothingness she appeared from.

It is anyone's guess why she only began appearing after the West tunnel was completed or why she is never seen above ground where her body was found. Perhaps the purpose of her apparition is to remind students of the luxury they enjoy in a tunnel system that never existed when she was alive. Or she may be staging some sort of protest, angry that the West tunnel did not exist when she was attending the university. If it had, the young student would probably still be alive today. Either way, her spirit appears less and less often, and when she does materialize in the passage between West Hall and Wilkerson, she appears more faintly—sometimes so transparent that she is almost indiscernible from the tunnel she is floating in. We can only hope that she has come to accept the tragic circumstances of her death and is fading into a peaceful oblivion as the vicious winter night that claimed her grows more distant.

INDIANA
Return of the Gipper

This story is a selection from Edrick Thay's Ghost Stories of Indiana.

One of the most famous residents of the University of Notre Dame's Washington Hall was—and perhaps still is—sports legend George Gipp.

Gipp, possibly the greatest all-round player in college football history, was a varsity athlete at Notre Dame from 1917 to 1920. He lived in Washington Hall the entire time. And according to Mark Marimen, author of *Haunted Indiana*, his spirit may reside in the dormitory still.

Gipp was born on February 18, 1895, in Laurium, Michigan. He was the seventh of eight children and, by all accounts, a natural athlete. He had speed and agility and a competitive fire that burned brightly.

In 1916, Gipp headed to Notre Dame with ambitions of playing baseball. But one afternoon Knute Rockne, the coach of the Fighting Irish, spotted him drop-kicking a football 60

Washington Hall, home of George Gipp's mischievous ghost

and 70 yards just for the fun of it. The persuasive coach convinced Gipp to go out for his team instead.

Gipp experienced nothing but success on the gridiron. In fact, he proved to be the most versatile player Rockne ever had. He could run, pass and punt. He led his team to 20 consecutive wins and 2 Western Championships. But sadly, his career was cut short.

Playing against Indiana University in 1920, Gipp began to feel ill with a sore throat and chills. He lay in bed for a week, hoping to improve, and rose again only to compete against

Northwestern University. He played exceptionally well that game, but observers could see that he was ailing.

On November 23, Gipp was admitted to St. Joseph's Hospital and diagnosed with pneumonia and a serious streptococcic infection of the throat. Despite treatment, his condition worsened. Finally, on December 12, his family and Rockne were sent for. It was then that Gipp, already feeling the cold grip of death, famously implored his coach to "win one for the Gipper."

Two days later, Gipp lapsed into a coma and died. On December 17, the entire student body of Notre Dame came out to watch his casket being loaded onto a train for Calumet, Michigan. But while his body rests forever in Calumet, some say his spirit remains in South Bend.

Early in 1921, Jim Clancy was practicing his trumpet in Washington Hall's music room when he heard a strange, eerie sound resembling a low moan coming from the other side of the chamber. Startled, he got up and tried to locate the source of the noise. He found it in a tuba stacked along the wall.

Clancy approached the tuba, and immediately the moaning stopped. Thoroughly spooked, Clancy grabbed his music and began to rush out of the room. But before he could exit the chamber, he was stopped in his tracks, for the instrument began playing again.

Within days, other residents of Washington Hall also heard the unearthly sound. Joe Shanahan, sneaking back into the building one night, passed the band room as he headed for the staircase. At that exact time, a low moan broke the silence. Shanahan, his breath caught in his throat, slowly turned towards the sound. Immediately, he caught a glimpse of what he called a "gossamer haze." Terrified, he fled to his room.

As the weeks and months wore on, the moans became more and more common. And they began to be accompanied by the sound of footsteps. Students started to whisper about doors closing on their own and things disappearing from their rooms. And one person even reported that a ghost pushed him while he walked down the stairs.

In the mid-1970s, after some people claimed to have seen the spirit of George Gipp riding on horseback on the steps of Washington Hall, a group of curious students decided to launch a ghostly investigation. The students had heard the stories and were determined to prove the phenomenon's existence.

Armed with cameras and recording devices, the students broke into the hall. They were trying to be discreet, but were unable to set up their equipment in the dark, so they had to turn on the lights. But the lights wouldn't stay lit. The light switch flicked itself off immediately after it was flicked on.

Other odd things happened, too. Flashes from cameras began to fire on their own, and the air was filled with a mournful wail. Eventually, the students were filled with terror and ran away. They'd definitely found what they were looking for.

But although that particular group of students was frightened, it didn't seem as though the ghost was intent on scaring those who entered Washington Hall. In the late 1970s, a group of theater students with an interest in the paranormal decided to stay late in the building and hold a seance in an attempt to contact the spirit. They used a Ouija board and asked whether or not there was a spirit in the hall who wanted to speak with them. They received a puzzling, cryptic message: "SG—Good bye."

Confused, the students asked the question again. They got the same result. Uneasy about the situation, the budding thespians packed up and left. They heard footsteps behind them and, once outside, they dove into the bushes. Seconds later, a Notre Dame security guard stepped from the building. According to Marimen, the students claim to this day that SG stood for security guard, and that the spirit that walked the staircases of Washington Hall had been offering up a warning.

Today Washington Hall serves as the university theater. And those who occupy its rooms and offices claim that if the building was ever haunted, it certainly isn't now. Regardless, the mere mention of the name George Gipp continues to bring to mind the young man's life, his stellar football career and, of course, the possibility that he continues to cause mischief in his old stomping grounds from far beyond the grave.

VERMONT
Converse Hall

From the moment he enrolled in the University of Vermont's medical program, Henry L. Means was haunted by a nagging fear that he was in over his head. He had been attending all his classes, submitting all his assignments and receiving As in every exam he had written, but his irrational insecurity persisted. He coddled this fear every day and late into each night until it became his own personal demon. When he wasn't lost in overwhelming anxiety, the young medical student was poring over his textbooks. His obsession with failure became his defining personality trait, and almost all his time was spent in self-imposed isolation. While everyone else was reveling in collegiate debauchery, Henry was in his room, sweating over his notes until he fell into feverish, angst-ridden sleep.

Completely friendless and with a tenuous grasp on reality, Means felt his world crash down around him on the day he discovered that he had failed one of his December exams. The F scrawled on his paper might as well have been a death sentence. Who can say how many of us would be able to cope with the realization of our worst fear? How much would such an experience alter our character? Would we even survive? Thankfully, these are questions that most of us will never have to contend with. But for Means, the sight of his own monster rearing its ugly head was too much. On a dark January night, he made his way up to the attic of his dormitory, his failed exam in one hand, a noose in the other. He was discovered the following morning hanging by the neck from one of the attic beams, his F paper lying beneath his swaying feet.

Ever since Means was found in the attic of Converse Hall on that cold January morning in 1920, the old building has never been the same. And while the University of Vermont continues to graduate thousands of students every year, the one tortured soul who took his own life there does not seem able or willing to leave the institution that spelled his death with a single letter.

The University of Vermont was established in Burlington in 1791, a stone's throw from historic Lake Champlain. The fifth college chartered in New England, the university would eventually distinguish itself as a pioneer for libertarian reform. Taking an early stance for freedom of religion, the University of Vermont was also one of the first universities to admit female students. By 1875, Vermont's Phi Beta Kappa chapter became the first honor society in the country that permitted women to join. In 1877, the same society set another milestone by becoming the first to admit African-American students.

For most students who attend the University of Vermont, these facts are relegated to background information, in the same category as Betsy Ross, Thomas Edison and Henry

Ford—historical footnotes in the minds of young people who look more to the future than the past. But it is the small tragedy of Henry Means, tucked away in the recesses of the respected university's past, which continues to remind students in Converse Hall that their university was conceived in, and largely belongs to, another time.

Not that the architecture of Converse Hall fails to convey the antiquity of the student residence. It is an enormous gothic structure, with two gigantic wings flanking the main entrance and row upon row of windows that seem to stare out from looming brick walls. One of those buildings that is difficult to take in with a single glance, Converse Hall demands attention. Many who have lived in the student residence know that more than its majestic construction is remarkable. These University of Vermont students are intimately familiar with the disconsolate spirit of Henry Means, who after all the loneliness of his mortal years, finally seems willing to socialize with his fellow students.

The strange accounts by students living in Converse Hall began shortly after young Means was buried. Residents have been frightened half to death by the sound of footsteps down an empty hallway. The building lights suddenly acquired the disquieting tendency to flicker on and off, while doors will suddenly open or slam shut, without a trace of a draft to motivate them; rocking chairs have been known to begin oscillating with no visible person sitting in them. The ghost seems to have a particular dislike for alcohol, sending beer cans flying across the room during dormitory get-togethers that might have gotten a little bit out of hand.

These are the common accounts, which have occurred with such frequency over the years that they've become embedded in the local folklore. But there are two other, more eerie events that are told in much more hushed voices.

One of these events involves typewriters and began occurring sometime in the 1950s. On a cold January evening a faculty member was woken from sleep by the sound of his typewriter click-clacking away. He was alone in his room, so we might imagine the initial shock the man felt at hearing there was someone in his quarters at this hour, using his typewriter no less. Whatever fear he might have felt at the idea of an intruder was compounded when he rolled over to discover that there was no one sitting at his desk; the keys on the typewriter were moving by themselves, as if an invisible person were typing frantically. The instructor got up slowly and moved toward his desk, feeling goosebumps as he strained to get a look at what the phantom writer was typing. When he got close enough to the sheet of paper, he saw that it was churning out a string of chemical formulas and complex biology notes at an astounding speed. The notes continued for about three-quarters of the page before the characters began spelling out garbled nonsense. The typing stopped at exactly the end of the page. Years after, residents in Converse Hall would report the sound of typewriters going in the middle of the night, but never since has there been a paper in the typewriter that was recording the work of the ghostly student.

There is another event that occurs regularly enough to stay alive in the annals of student lore and that makes many students apprehensive about spending too much time in front of the mirror. Unlike the activity around the typewriters, the occurrences near the Converse Hall mirrors began soon after Means was found dead in the attic. No one knows who saw him first, the sallow young face in place of the familiar reflection, staring blankly at the horrified onlooker. Invariably, the vision in the mirror would only last for a few seconds before the mirror would become unfastened from the wall and fall crashing to the floor.

There isn't much doubt as to whose reflection this is. But why, exactly, Henry Means would choose to terrify his peers with these appearances is another question. Perhaps the young student was more lonely than he was stressed over his schoolwork; maybe his inability to connect with his classmates made him turn to his books with such singular devotion. A mortal fear of failure or a profound loneliness? The question will probably never be answered, but it is likely that both these fears worked in the poor man's mind, impelling him to do what he did. And perhaps continue to impel him to do what he does today.

While sightings of Henry's reflection in Converse Hall mirrors have trailed off in recent years, some students still feel an inexplicable chill when they are standing in front of a mirror. We can only hope Henry Means is getting over his earthly suffering and is finally moving on to whatever is waiting beyond, away from the dark halls of Converse Hall that caused him so much torment while he was alive.

8
Frightening Folklore

NEVADA
The Ghost of Eilley Bowers

Alison "Eilley" Oram was *the* grande dame of early Nevada. An early settler in the Washoe Valley, she was one of the extraordinary women of western America, winning and losing her fortune by the tumultuous boom and bust conditions of the mining frontier. Born in Scotland on September 6, 1826, Eilley married when she was 15 and moved to the Great Salt Lake soon after with Stephen Hunter, her devoutly Mormon husband. It would be the last time she rode on the coattails of any man.

In a time when divorce was not a realistic option for so many women, young Eilley left her husband soon after they arrived in America; the reasons behind this separation are forgotten by history, but whatever they were, they did not spoil the idea of marriage for the Scot. She married another Mormon named Alexander Cowan in 1853. Two years later, man and wife moved to what is now Nevada. Acting as Mormon missionaries, the two set up a ranch near present-day Genoa, moving on to the Washoe Valley in western Nevada about one year later. While Eilley was already an anomaly among women in her willingness to settle on the rough fringes of American civilization, she became one of the legendary figures of the region when she decided to stay behind in the Washoe Valley after her husband was called back to Utah by the Mormon order.

She effectively ended her marriage to Alexander Cowan, and it was not long before she was rewarded for her bold independence. Moving south to a small mining camp called Johntown, she set up a boarding house, supplying miners with decent rooms in a rough settlement where tents were the common shelter. The move was fortuitous. In 1859, gold was discovered on a nearby hill, and miners rushed into the region, bringing a suddenly booming business to the enterprising young woman. She was not content to live off the earnings of the miners, however, and soon got involved in mining herself. Living in the region before the rush of miners began, Eilley had her pick of the mining plots along Gold Hill. One of her claims bordered on another claim owned by one Lemuel "Sandy" Bowers. The handsome young Scotsman developed a deep admiration for Eilley's dauntless ambition, and the two were wed under fortunate auspices, as both their claims began churning out incredible amounts of wealth.

Eilley and Sandy Bowers became Nevada's first two millionaires. Tapping into the enormous Comstock Lode, the couple became the recipients of more money than they had ever dared to imagine. This abundance of cash greased the wheels of their nuptial arrangements, and a true and lasting love formed between them. But with greater wealth came greater potential for tragedy: the more one has, the more one has to lose. Fortune's familiar pattern of generous bestowal and cruel deprivation did not spare the Bowers. The twists of fate Eilley would suffer throughout the rest of her days turned her attention to mystical forces, and she spent the last years of her life engrossed in the spirit world, looking to the spirits of the underworld for guidance—until she became one of those spirits herself.

The Bowers' impending misfortunes arrived along with their first two children, who both died in their infancy. Perhaps the Bowers were seeking some respite from the sorrow of these losses when they commissioned their mansion to be built and took off on a 10-month trip through Europe. They came back to their newly constructed mansion along with a child whom they had adopted somewhere in the

Scottish highlands; Eilley was never forthcoming about the girl's background.

But the Bowers would not have much time to enjoy any familial happiness. Soon after they returned, their mines began to run out. Outstanding debts suddenly loomed large before the Bower family, and their savings and income rapidly deteriorated. By the time Sandy went to their mines on Gold Hill to oversee the operation, the ore had all but run out. Poverty, however, was not an issue Mr. Bower had to contend with for too long. With a broken heart and lungs full of rock dust, Sandy died of silicosis early in 1868.

Eilley was alone again, doing everything she could to raise her adopted daughter in a world that was decidedly hostile to independent women. She turned her mansion into a boarding house in hopes of paying off her debts, but her efforts were in vain. She became more removed from reality as her fortunes plummeted, yet it was in 1874, when her daughter died after her appendix burst in a Reno boarding school, that Eilley's worldview changed dramatically.

She lost her mansion in a public auction in 1876 and spent the rest of her life dabbling in the spirit world, making a meager living looking into her crystal ball, giving superstitious clients a look into their futures for a small price. She also claimed she could communicate with spirits of the departed and charged to deliver messages to clients' deceased loved ones. After wandering between California and Nevada, the once incredibly wealthy mine proprietor spent her last days in an Oakland, California, poorhouse. She died on October 27, 1903.

But that would not be the last the world would hear of Eilley Bowers. Strange things began to happen in the Bowers Mansion soon after she passed away. There were reports of mysterious sounds coming from deserted hallways and rooms. People described them as shuffling sounds; objects were being moved about, as if someone was looking for a missing possession, emptying closets, nightstands and dressers. But investigations never revealed any intruder, just an empty, rearranged chamber.

Other people claimed to see a stately-looking matriarch dressed in Victorian splendor standing stoically before one of the mansion's windows, looking out on the estate's sprawling grounds. The woman was described as broad, with short dark hair and hard features, descriptions that match the portraits of the same legendary entrepreneur who had the mansion built.

These sightings have increased dramatically since the Bower Mansion was opened for tours. Many believe Eilley is returning for her crystal ball, which is displayed in the mansion today. Others think that her spirit is reliving those few days of happiness when she was living in the mansion with her daughter and husband, before the cruel hands of fate tore their household apart.

IOWA
Emma Schmidt

The people of Earling, Iowa, remember it still. They remember as if it happened only yesterday. While some in this community of 466 were not alive to witness firsthand the events that took place in September 1928, they too remember. They have heard the stories, the words leaving indelible marks on conscience, soul and memory. Some might question the truth about what happened during that fateful September but no less an authority than the Vatican has documented the event. After all, as related by Beth Scott and Michael Norman in *Haunted Heartland*, it's not every day that the devil pays a visit to your town.

From the time of her father's death when she was just 14, Emma Schmidt hadn't felt like herself. She found herself overwhelmed by a hatred for almost everything, even close family and friends, and confused by an inability to understand both her actions and her words. Most perplexing of all was her behavior in church as obscenities and a volley of inhuman cries, growls and moans issued forth from her foaming mouth, tearing through the hallowed service.

Emma's family took the girl to doctors and specialists throughout the state but none had the ability to end Emma's suffering. An appeal was made to the Catholic Church. If the solution could not be found in the secular, perhaps then it would be found in the spiritual.

Over a number of years, through which Emma endured increasing pain and confusion, priests observed the girl. They acted slowly, purposefully, suspecting the worst but praying for the best. She understood languages that she had neither heard nor read. When priests blessed her in Latin, she began foaming at the mouth. Objects sprinkled with holy water elicited the same reaction. In hushed tones, priests discussed Emma Schmidt's condition, almost unwilling to speak aloud their suspicions, as if their thoughts would be a stain on silence, as if they would transmute the abstract into the concrete. But the truth wouldn't be denied. Emma was possessed, with a mind that had been overtaken by the devil himself, and an exorcism was necessary for her total liberation.

Great care had to be taken in deciding who would perform the exorcism—a girl's life and salvation hung in the balance. The exorcist must be humble and courageous, relying on God alone for direction and guidance while fearing not the devil and his demons. The exorcist must have integrity, the ability to turn from the seductive path of temptation and to persevere in the face of near overwhelming adversity. For the Catholic priests dealing with Emma's case, the choice was clear.

Father Theophilus Reisinger was a Capuchin monk and exorcist from Marathon, Wisconsin. The Capuchins, an order of Franciscan monks established at the beginning of the Catholic Reformation in the early 16th century, were especially devoted to austerity and poverty and had played an instrumental role in reviving Catholicism in parts of Europe where Protestantism had taken root. A number of them participated in early foreign missions to Canada and the United States. This dedication to creed in the face of suffocating opposition and resistance from both Protestants in Europe and aboriginals in North America marked the Capuchins as true men of the cloth, men who would not bend or break. Father Reisinger was thus particularly suited to exorcising Emma Schmidt's demons. A lesser man might very well have failed. Emma's exorcism would prove difficult.

Father Reisinger sought to protect Emma's privacy and contacted the convent of the Franciscan sisters in the village of Earling, a small community of primarily German immigrants and farmers located in the gently rolling hills of Iowa. The village was located in the parish of an old friend, Joseph Steiger. Father Steiger resisted the idea, reluctant to expose his parishioners to this brand of terror. However, the convent's Mother Superior was more than willing to accommodate Father Reisinger and on the first of September, Emma arrived in Earling.

Her arrival was not without incident. Greeted by sisters from the convent, Emma screamed obscenities and threatened the nuns before collapsing. Pastor Steiger's reluctance was not diminished when he set out to pick Father Reisinger up from the train station. Even though Steiger was driving a new car, his vehicle stalled again and again. At other times, it would lurch across the road as if possessed, placing the pastor in very real danger as his car careened its way through traffic. A journey that normally took just minutes to complete stretched out for over two hours as Pastor Steiger struggled to maintain control over his car.

He arrived at the train station, further convinced that bringing Emma Schmidt to Earling was a mistake. Father Reisinger dismissed the pastor's words. He had suspected that the devil might attempt to intervene on the behalf of those possessing Emma's mind. Before getting into Pastor Steiger's car, he blessed the car with the sign of the cross and recited the rosary as they made their way towards the convent. They arrived shortly thereafter.

Emma, on the other hand, was raising a bit of a ruckus at the convent, refusing all attempts to feed her. The floor was littered with the remnants of the nuns' efforts, trays and food scattered about like so much confetti. Only after the sisters stopped blessing the food did Emma eat. Father Reisinger took everything in stride; he knew that here was only the beginning. Before it was over, the resolve of everyone involved would be tested; their combined strength and endurance would be stretched to their limits.

To begin, Father Reisinger placed Emma on an iron bed. He tied down her hands and legs and then instructed the nuns to hold her body down. But before they could, they found themselves watching with a strange mixture of fear and awe as Emma's body was thrown from the bed as if by an unseen force and pinned against the wall. The nuns grabbed at her feet but Emma skittered out of their grasps until one managed to lay hold of an ankle. Emma was pulled back down, and again, Father Reisinger strapped down her limbs. The nuns moved quickly, throwing their collective strength against Emma to prevent her body from launching itself through the air again. The move displeased the spirits within; from deep within her stomach came an unearthly howl, guttural and primal, so disturbing that residents of Earling came running to the convent to see what was happening. Most departed within moments, unable to stomach Emma's screams. Those who stayed left soon after as Emma began frothing at the mouth and proceeded to vomit repeatedly.

Many days of the same behavior followed, but Father Reisinger was not deterred. Little by little, he progressed. Soon, he had determined that a number of spirits were inhabiting Emma's body, that among them was Beelzebub himself as well as Judas Iscariot. Her father's mistress was inside as well, a wretch of a woman who was condemned to an eternity in hell for murdering her own children. Further investigation revealed that Emma's father, Jacob, possessed her too. Father Reisinger was intrigued by this presence; why was Emma's father possessing her body?

He was appalled to learn that it was Emma's father, Jacob, who had cursed her. Unable to resist the darkest and most perverse of his desires, he had prayed for devils to come and take her body, to destroy her body and soul. The devil, it seemed, had answered his prayers. Jacob's reasons for tormenting his daughter must remain a mystery. Love, that greatest and purest of emotions, is subject to degradation and perversion, just like anything else.

A transition also came over Pastor Steiger. Granted, Pastor Steiger and Father Reisinger had been separated by distance and time, but those two dimensions could not break the bonds of true friendship. But in Earling, Pastor Steiger began to doubt Father Reisinger's ability, allowing a hatred for the entire enterprise to fester and spread. He resented how the procedure was affecting Earling. Pastor Steiger's animosity increased with every day Emma lay strapped to the bed. He issued forth torrents of vitriol, determined to denounce both the operation and Father Reisinger. While others might have been shocked at the speed with which Pastor Steiger turned on his old friend, Father Reisinger suggested to the priest that the devil was influencing him, as he had Jacob Schmidt, using him to impede the exorcism. To resist, the father asked the priest to place his faith in God, to remember all that is good and holy, to believe in love's purity and power.

His faith was a necessity for Emma, the poor girl who had been cursed by the very man who was meant to protect her. As Emma lay there on her iron bed, she needed something to fix her resolve on. Her suffering was tremendous. Despite her repeated vomiting, her body had begun to swell. Her eyes bulged from their sockets and her lips ballooned to twice their size. At times, her body became so heavy that the iron bed shuddered under the weight. Pastor Steiger needed, more than ever, to maintain his faith. The devil realized this necessity.

Through Emma, the devil warned Pastor Steiger that he'd have to be careful on the following Friday. That Friday, the pastor received a call from a farmer begging him to perform last rites for his dying mother. Pastor Steiger left for the home and, with the devil's warning in mind, prayed to Saint Joseph to protect him from harm. Saint Joseph listened and acted when Pastor Steiger's car crashed on a bridge, careened through the guardrail and stopped just short of dropping into the gaping chasm below. Shaken emotionally, Pastor Steiger walked away from the accident without injury.

That night, the pastor was tormented in his bedroom by the persistent noise of what sounded like thousands of mice scurrying across the floor and through the walls. Pastor Steiger, aroused from slumber, lit two candles before a crucifix and recited a short prayer of exorcism. With that act, silence descended upon the room. Pastor Steiger was able to sleep in peace for the next little while but then one night, his very house began to shake and roll. He leapt out of bed, but when he tried to open his bedroom door, he found it resisted his attempts. He was trapped; the quake stopped only when he recited the exorcism again and sprinkled the room with holy water. Steiger, bolstered by Father Reisinger's support, did not falter this time. He would not run from his fears; they would not become his enemy. He saw now how fear could manipulate him, how fear was allied with evil and how Emma needed him to be strong. As it was, she was growing weaker with each passing day.

Exorcisms did not take place overnight. That much was understood when the process began in Earling. But no one could have predicted that almost a month would pass before there was any indication that Emma's demons would be exorcised. Regardless, Father Reisinger pressed on and at the first moment of weakness, he attacked. He spent the next three days working, forgoing sleep and rest, until the last of his strength had ebbed, until he was so weak with exhaustion he was forced to pray to God so that his life might be spared. To support Reisinger's efforts, Pastor Steiger asked his parishioners to keep regular hours of adoration before the Blessed Virgin, to fast and do penance. This the people of Earling did for days, until the fateful day that a nun saw a cluster of white roses on the ceiling of Emma's room. The nuns saw it as a sign that the end was near, that soon, Emma would both be purged of her demons and be purified and blessed with the love and innocence of the Virgin Mary. Redemption was at hand.

On September 23, 1928, at nine in the evening, Emma jerked free from the nuns' grasp and stood on the bed. Then, she collapsed. Father Reisinger demanded that the devils give a sign of their departure by calling out their names. Disembodied voices rang out, calling Beelzebub, Judas, Jacob and Mina. Emma awoke a short time later, pure once more of heart and spirit. Father Reisinger and Pastor Steiger had succeeded.

It's said that Emma lived the rest of her life in peace and calm. While there are those who question whether demonic possession can occur, for the people of Earling, Iowa, that is a question that can only be answered in the resoundingly positive.

TENNESSEE
The Bell Witch

The stories may be old, but the mysteries surrounding the Bell Witch continue to confound the people of Robertson County even today, because what happened nearly 200 years ago defies all logic and offers a glimpse into that world at the edge of reason, a world where something lurks within every shadow. For the Bells of Tennessee, that something was the Bell Witch, an apparition dedicated to tormenting and torturing the family, especially its patriarch, John, and daughter, Betsy. So pervasive was the witch's presence that she captured the attention of people all across Tennessee. Those who encountered her spoke about her in hushed tones; those who disbelieved were not skeptics for long. The Bell Witch was persuasive.

When the Bell Witch first appeared in 1817, the Bells couldn't know the dark and twisted path the witch would lead them on. After all, when she began to make her presence felt, all she did was indulge in what seemed to be good-natured fun—sugar disappeared from bowls, milk was spilled, quilts vanished only to reappear in different places. Her tricks called to mind nothing more than a child's pranks. They were dismissed and forgotten. But these were only the prelude to what would be a symphony of terror.

Who exactly was the Bell Witch? Nobody seems to know. Some speculate that she once loved John Bell, but he spurned her advances. When he married, she refused to leave him alone in his wedded bliss. At wits' end, Bell lured the woman over to his house and murdered her, so great was his desperation. Before she died, she promised to haunt him until his death. Another account paints the woman as a victim of

A detail of a painting of the Battle of New Orleans shows Andrew Jackson, who said he'd rather fight the British than the Bell Witch.

Bell's questionable land dealings while another has her on the short end of a slave exchange. These theories seem to agree that her name was Kate Batts, that she had been wronged somehow by John Bell and that she would not rest until she had her revenge.

Not content with providing simple irritations, the spirit began a campaign of physical abuse, kicking, scratching, slapping and pinching various family members. Some days, the witch scratched John's leg until it bled. Betsy's blankets were pulled from her bed as quickly as she could replace them and while she slept she was stuck with pins and often woke in the morning with bruises running the length of her body. When the witch's victims cried out in pain, she responded with a shrill and frightful screech, clearly taking pleasure in her victims' suffering.

News of the strange events on the Bell farm spread from county to county, and people came hoping to catch a glimpse of the unusual. Many reported having conversations with the spirit, that she could be gentle and had a melodic voice. It seems that the witch reserved her worst for the Bells and those who doubted her powers. One of those skeptics was General Andrew Jackson, the man who would be the seventh president of the United States.

According to accounts, the Bell men had fought under Jackson in the Battle of New Orleans; they were close, men whose camaraderie had been forged in the fires of war. While in Nashville, Jackson heard about what was happening in Robertson County. Organizing a party, Jackson and his men set out on horseback to see the Bell Witch for themselves. As they approached Bells' farm, they boasted about what they would do to the witch if she should confront them, how they would chase her away and rid Robertson County of her menace for good. It was all in vain, of course; these men, whose wills had been tempered by physical combat, were ill-prepared to oppose a being who took no physical form.

No sooner had Jackson uttered his intentions than his wagon stopped abruptly, though the road was smooth and level, free of ruts or potholes. Jackson spurred the horses on with the lash but as much as they strained and pulled, the wagon would not move. The horses struggled and fought, but they soon tired, the wagon having given not even an inch. Jackson gave up and is said to have proclaimed that it was the witch. She apparently answered, claiming that she would now let them go, but would return to them later that night. The wagon began to move.

That night, while sleeping in the Bells' barn, Jackson had his covers ripped from his pallet, and the entire party was subjected to the slapping, pinching and hair-pulling that the Bells experienced so often. Jackson left soon after, saying that he would rather fight the British in New Orleans than the Bell Witch in Tennessee.

Unfortunately, it was not so easy for the Bells to escape the witch. Try as he might, John could not escape her wrath. He moved from one home to another, only to find a precious few days of peace before the witch arrived again to visit her unique brand of hospitality. Despite three years of constant suffering, the worst was yet to come for the Bells.

In October 1820, John fell ill. Some speculate he suffered a stroke as he had trouble speaking and swallowing soon after. Regardless, one morning, John was found in bed in a deep stupor. Try as they might, his family could not rouse him into consciousness. His breath had a foul odor. Concerned, his son Jesse went to the medicine cabinet to retrieve his father's medication only to find that it had been replaced with a strange-looking vial filled with a viscous fluid that smelled very much the same as his father's breath. With quivering hand and nervous heart, Jesse asked his family about the vial. No one had any idea where it might have come from but they feared it might be poisonous. A single drop was fed to the family cat; the animal dropped dead almost instantly. The Bells' collective gasp was overwhelmed by a maniacal cackle; it was a familiar laugh. The witch's shrill voice rent the air, and she took credit for the vial, saying that she had used the liquid inside to kill John. Indeed, during the fuss over the mysterious vial, John passed away. John Bell was buried days later and while the ceremony was relatively free from interruptions, as soon as the grave had been filled, the Bell Witch returned, filling the air with gleeful laughter.

Soon after, she left the family, promising that she would return in seven years. She did, visiting John Bell, Jr., for about a month. Before she left, historians believe she left Bell, Jr. with prophecies that predicted the coming of the Civil War as well as the First and Second World Wars. Again, she promised to return, only this time it would be in 135 years. No one knows if the Bell Witch ever returned to haunt the Bells' descendants but there are those in Robertson County who believe that the witch is now roaming the lands in and around Adams, Tennessee. If you believe the whispers, strange things are still happening out on the old Bell farmstead.

WEST VIRGINIA
The Stranger

Adam Livingston and his family led a quiet life on a large farm in York County, Pennsylvania. He had a beautiful wife, three sons and four daughters. Livingston wanted nothing more. But then strange things began happening on his farm. A mysterious fire claimed his barn and then an epidemic leveled his stock of horses and cattle. Decimated by bad fortune, Livingston determined that a change of location was the only way. So in the early 1790s, he moved to Virginia, bought 70 acres of land and settled in Smithfield, near what is present-day Middleway, West Virginia.

The family's new neighbors embraced the family warmly, and Livingston acquired a reputation as a hard-working farmer who was bright and honest. Some muttered darkly, however, about Livingston's devotion to Lutheranism, one so full and complete that Livingston came to be known also as a bigot who disdained all other religions. But, for the most part, the family lived a quiet, innocuous life—that is, until the day the stranger came.

In 1794, a stranger, described in a 1904 *West Virginia Historical Magazine Quarterly* as "of middle age and of respectable appearance," stopped at the Livingston homestead and asked for accommodations. His wagon had lost a wheel and he needed a warm place to spend the night. But it soon became apparent that the man had wanted more than just a warm bed. He was seeking a place to die. As the night passed, the man's condition only worsened; realizing that death was near, the stranger asked Livingston to seek out a Catholic priest to give him his last rites. Livingston refused. He knew no Catholic priest and even if he had, he would never allow one in his home. The dying man repeated his request, but Livingston remained adamant. No Catholic priest was going to enter his Lutheran home. The stranger had no choice but to die. Livingston never bothered to learn the identity of the visitor; a quick search of the man's papers revealed no name. Having suffered the indignity of dying without his last rites, the stranger would now be buried in a potter's field with nothing to mark his passing. But from the moment the stranger died, strange things began happening in the home—occurrences Livingston could only attribute to the spirit of the dead.

Livingston asked a friend, Jacob Foster, to watch over the corpse for the evening before its burial the following day. Foster accepted the task but fled the house when candles kept extinguishing themselves in the room. Livingston resolved to bury the body at earliest light to eliminate what he judged to be the source of Foster's fear. After the burial, however, Livingston's problems only multiplied.

The family was tormented nightly by sounds of galloping horses and knocks on the door, only no one ever saw the horses or the person at the door. The sounds came from nowhere. As the weeks passed, the events progressed from petty annoyances to serious problems. Livingston's animals began dying. Pottery in the house would throw itself to the floor, as if hurtled by unseen hands. Chunks of burning logs would leap from the fireplace, threatening to ignite the Livingston home. And, most disturbing of all, sounds of scissors snipping and clipping filled the house. Shortly after, members of the Livingston family were stunned and shocked to find blankets, sheets, boots and clothing cut to shreds. The sound of clipping never ceased. It continued every minute of every hour of every day.

News soon spread throughout the county of the eerie events taking place on the Livingston homestead. Some believed that the reports were nothing more than elaborate hoaxes; others set out for Smithfield to test their assumptions. A woman came wearing a new silk cap that she took off before she entered the home. She wrapped it in a silk hand-kerchief and put the package in her pocket, determined to foil the phantom shears. Yet after she left the home and inspected the hat, she was flabbergasted to find the cap in shreds.

The situation grew desperate. Livingston's health was beginning to fail and the stress threatened to overwhelm his sanity. He called upon three professional conjurers to cast spells on his home and rid it of its presence, but their incan-tations proved futile. Livingston was devastated and he gave up hope of ever finding a solution. Then, one night, he had a vision. He saw a man in robes and heard a voice that told him, "This is the man who can relieve you." When he awoke, he was determined to find the robed man.

With the help of friends in Shepherdsville, Livingston managed to track down the man from his dreams. When Livingston first saw him, he was overcome by his vision rendered real. The man who appeared to Livingston in a dream was now standing in his home. The man was Father Cahill, a Catholic priest. Livingston was so desperate that he admitted the man into his home, allowing now what he had determined was impossible for a dying man.

Initially, Father Cahill doubted Livingston's claims, but a visit to the homestead and Smithfield convinced the priest that there was indeed something unnatural taking place. Cahill uttered some prayers and then sprinkled the home with holy water. After he left, the Livingstons waited anx-iously for night to come, to see if they would, at long last, pass one evening undisturbed.

That evening, the Livingstons slept soundly for the first time in months. And so it was for the next couple of evenings until one day when the weird noises and dreadful clipping began anew. Cahill returned. This time, he celebrated mass and consecrated the dead stranger's burial plot. With that, the disturbances stopped for good.

Livingston soon converted to Catholicism, and for years thereafter he heard a voice that prayed with the family, advised them and offered predictions for the future. In 1802, Livingston deeded a portion of his property to the Catholic Church after the voice told him, "Before the end of time, this will be a great place of prayer and fasting and praise."

Today, the plot of land supports the Priestfield Pastoral Center, a place for prayer, fasting and praise. Although the Livingstons lived out the rest of their days in relative peace, the same cannot be said for the spirit. Not nearly as restless as he once was, he can occasionally be seen disappearing into the Catholic chapel on the old Livingston property on autumn nights. Tourists visiting the site have sometimes found their purse and camera straps mysteriously cut. Old habits, it seems, die hard.

～ The Spooky End ～

Story Locations

Enjoy more haunting tales in these collections by

GHOST HOUSE

GHOST HOUSE BOOKS

The colorful history of North America includes many spine-tingling tales of the supernatural. These fun, fascinating books by GHOST HOUSE BOOKS reveal the rich diversity of haunted places on the continent. Our ghostly tales involve well-known theatres, buildings and other landmarks, many of which are still in use. Collect the whole series!

Ghost Stories of Ohio *by Edrick Thay*

Visit the ghosts of America's heartland with this volume of paranormal accounts from Ohio. A stop at the Buxton Inn could yield a glimpse of one of its spirited guests. Tour Athens, reportedly one of the world's most haunted places. Discover the town of Wooster, which got back more than just an antique when it retrieved an ancient steam pumper.
$10.95 • ISBN 1-894877-09-8 • 5.25" x 8.25" • 200 pages

Ghost Stories of Michigan *by Dan Asfar*

This spirited collection features ghost stories from throughout the Great Lakes State, such as the Red Dwarf of Detroit, who turns up whenever tragedy visits, and the ghostly lighthouse keeper of White River who continues to warn of danger.
$10.95 • ISBN 1-894877-05-5 • 5.25" x 8.25" • 224 pages

Ghost Stories of Indiana *by Edrick Thay*

This fascinating collection of paranormal folklore from the Hoosier State includes the story of the original "Gipper," George Gipp, who is said to still roam the halls of the University of Notre Dame, where he was a football star. Among many other tales is one about a restless spirit still searching for his little girl at Spook Light Hill near Terre Haute, while another tells of the haunting of Purdue University by the spirit of former instructor and renowned aviatrix Amelia Earhart.
$10.95 • ISBN 1-894877-06-3 • 5.25" x 8.25" • 200 pages

Ghost Stories of Pennsylvania *by Dan Asfar*

After close to four centuries of European settlement, complete with revolutionary and civil wars, Pennsylvania has an abundance of history and folklore. Dan Asfar has roamed the Keystone State in search of great ghost stories, to Pittsburgh, Philadelphia, Gettysburg, the Allegheny Mountains, Pennsylvania Dutch Country and the Poconos.
$10.95 • ISBN 1-894877-08-X • 5.25" x 8.25" • 200 pages

These and many more *Ghost Stories* books are available from your local bookseller or by ordering direct at 1-800-518-3541.